RUSSIA

An Illustrated History

RUSSIA

An Illustrated History

JOEL CARMICHAEL

HIPPOCRENE BOOKS INC.
NEW YORK

For information, address:
HIPPOCRENE BOOKS, INC.
171 Madison Avenue
New York, NY 10016

ISBN 0-7818-0689-5

Printed in the United States of America.

CONTENTS

FOREWORD

It is fashionable to distrust the sweep of generalization. Yet the temptation to extract a pattern from the thousand years of Russian history is irresistible.

Russia owes its germination to the vagaries of international trade: when Europe was barred from the Mediterranean by the expansion of Islam a thousand years ago, the Vikings—armed businessmen who had established a chain of trading posts between the Middle East and northern Europe—created the embryonic Russian State while bypassing the Middle East.

But this seminal contact was entirely exceptional: Russia generally remained isolated from contemporary influences. Cut off from Byzantium by the Tatars and Turks under the House of Chingis Khan, it was impinged on by a more advanced society only twice before the modern era—when Novgorod briefly led the Hanseatic League in the thirteenth to fifteenth century, and when English merchants found the North Sea route to Muscovy in 1553.

Urban growth, the groundwork of civilization, was inhibited in Russia by the interaction of two factors—remoteness from the international trade routes and the rural backwardness that prevented the accumulation of surpluses.

Russia's population remained small for centuries. In the mid-sixteenth century it numbered 9–11 million, at a time when France numbered 19 million, Spain 11, and Austria 20; in the following century Poland had about 11 million people.

As in Europe generally, but with a greater coefficient of increase, a demographic spurt began in Russia around 1750:

in a single century the population quadrupled—from 17–18 million to 68. By 1897 it numbered 124 million; in 1914,170 million. Today the Soviet Union has more than 250,000,000 people.

Russian evolution was framed by its general backwardness, its scanty population, its great expanse, and the vulnerability of its frontiers.

The characteristic institutions of the West may be said to stem from a differentiation, originating in Rome, between two types of authority—over people and over objects. It was this fundamental cleavage of category that ultimately enabled Western society to distinguish between statecraft and the management of property.

In Russia this complex development, slow to start, remained unconsummated. The Vikings who had launched Russia never settled down within juridical structures based on territory, as they did in England and Sicily, but persisted as a merchant community rather like the English East India Company or the Hudson's Bay Company in Canada. Owning their territory collectively, they required no constitutional differentiations. Thus in the very genesis of Russian society the confusion between ownership and sovereignty suffocated the conception of political authority.

The "patrimonial" mentality of the Vikings laid the foundations of authoritarianism, whose essence consists of just this lumping together of two distinct relationships. Russia has in fact remained the patrimonial state *par excellence:* Russian rulers have been both sovereigns of the realm and its proprietors. There was no foundation for an institution that in Western Europe was basic—contractual vassalage, which, entailing a network of reciprocal rights and duties, is the foundation of personal liberty as well as constitutionality.

The natural consequence of the absence of reciprocity was arbitrary force. Just as the absence of contractual vassalage gave rise to pervasive lawlessness in Russian society, so the lawlessness of society, conversely, engendered extravagant measures of repression to cope with it.

This had a further corollary: the struggle for liberty, lacking an anchorage in the self-consciousness of real social groupings, could not depend on accepted social norms, but was obliged to invoke abstract ideals. Thus two abstractions collided—arbitrary force and intellectual idealism.

As Russia's contacts with the West began proliferating a couple of centuries ago, this polarization grew more and more difficult to sustain. Indeed, the conflict between authoritarianism and the desire for liberty has generated a pervasive internal tension down to our own day.

The Russian state inevitably remained oppressive: in the absence of an instinct, so to speak, for constitutionality, the conflict between force and freedom became the matrix of society. In the nineteenth century the tradition of police rule, especially concentrated since Ivan the Terrible and Peter the Great, was further institutionalized. From 1845 on all criminal codes contained an "omnibus" clause worded so vaguely that the government could imprison anyone for such crimes as "undermining" morale or "arousing doubts" and "disrespect."

Against an age-old background the repression that characterized the second half of the nineteenth century was particularly stimulated by the shake-up of the elite: the educated classes—especially, of course, their idealistic children—were permeated by "liberal" and "revolutionary" sentiments. As dissidence was organized in the seventies and eighties, the government was bound to react: after the celebrated Zasulich case in 1878—in which a militant dissident, given a jury trial for shooting a high functionary, was freed by the pressure of "public opinion"—juries were avoided altogether and administrative methods were resorted to in handling the population.

Thus, by the early eighties, all elements of a bureaucratic-police regime were present—the police were preoccupied with crimes against the state; politics was the business of high functionaries. The security organs, authorized to search, arrest, imprison and exile anyone suspected of political activity, had, in theory, practically limitless control of the population.

Nevertheless, administrative repression was already slackening substantially in the late nineteenth and early twentieth century. The vitality of free enterprise, energetically reinforced by capital from Western Europe, was transforming society. The first translation of Karl Marx's *Capital* was into Russian Marx's notion that "capitalism" had to realize its full potential *before* it could be shaken, fitted in very appropriately with the large-scale organization of new industrial complexes: the railways alone were changing the face of Russia.

In addition, a powerful social force counterbalanced the administrative hangovers of the past. The Russian upper classes had sponged up European culture, especially in its French and German versions, with such avidity that by the end of the eighteenth century they were producing a first-rate intelligentsia, gifted and energetic in the arts and sciences, with able thinkers bestriding all horizons. In the nineteenth century cultivated Russians had become numerous enough to outweigh the patrimonial spirit infusing the regime's conception of itself.

The Tsarist administration never, for instance, violated property rights. Alexander Herzen, while in the midst of attacking the regime from the safety of London in his periodical *The Bell*, always had his personal revenues forwarded to him. Lenin's mother drew a government pension as a civil servant's widow even after one son had been executed for an attempt on the Tsar's life and two others had been jailed.

Upper class urbanity had even permeated the security organs, where cultivated gentlemen took a genuine interest in the ideas of the revolutionaries and treated them with remarkable indulgence. Life in Siberia was practically idyllic: revolutionaries could hunt, shoot, fish, read and write books, hold meetings, and escape at will.

Under the Tsars, Russian officialdom was rather small; moreover, the lack of funds, the size of the country, and the difficulties of communication combined to hamstring it. In the 1880s only 17 people were executed, all of them assassins or would-be assassins; during the repression under Alexander III that followed the assassination of his father, only 4,000 people were interrogated, in connection with genuine offenses.

With the Tsarist breakdown in 1917—from February to October—repression vanished totally; for eight months Russia was freer than ever before.

In October the Bolshevik nucleus took over the patrimonial idea in its purest form—it expropriated the whole country. Giving the center a matchlessly tight control by modernizing both transport and communications, it solved the bureaucratic problem of allocating funds between government departments—repression was now the very essence of the regime.

The temporary restoration of capitalism in 1921 that the parvenu regime was obliged to resort to by the twin disasters of "War Communism" and the Civil War played out its role of reviving the economy within the tight embrace of the streamlined despotism: it was brought to an abrupt end in 1929 by the crash programs of collectivization and industrialization that constituted the true Russian revolution. It was then that totalitarianism truly flowered.

What had been a mere potentiality under Tsarism was endlessly realized by the Bolshevik apparatus. The omnibus clauses of the Tsarist criminal codes reached full fruition in the Bolshevik codes of 1927 and 1960. The apparatus foreshadowed under Alexander III achieved a scope and ferocity unprecedented in history, consolidating itself in the thirties: at least 20 percent of the population were destroyed. By mid-twentieth century the Bolshevik conspiratorial nucleus had grown into an elite comprising some one percent of the population.

The first political action taken by the Bolsheviks after the *putsch* was to dissolve the Constituent Assembly, a political goal they had shared beforehand with generations of Russians. Thus the neo-Bolshevik dictatorship was in full control of all the resources of the State.

In addition, though Marxism does not, in fact, contain any guidance for societies after their transition to socialism or communism, and even though the very seizure of power by a socialist party in a backward peasant country contradicted the main thesis of Marxism, this could not be admitted, since it would have detracted from the authority of the new government. In fact, Marxism was turned into a State cult and taken as the foundation of all education and discourse: though the problems facing the new regime could not be solved by Marxism, it was to remain the idiom of the government; the inherent flexibility of that idiom was to serve as a vehicle for explanation, justification, and exhortation from then on. Thus the ideas of Rousseau, Hegel and Marx may be said to have achieved, through contradiction, an institutional expression.

The control of the State, plus the cult of "Marxist-Leninist" orthodoxy devised by Stalin, brought about a mixture of autocracy and sectarianism buttressed by technology, the most massive police state in history.

INTRODUCTION

The most obvious thing about Russia may also be the most illuminating: its sheer size. Encompassing one-sixth of the land surface of the earth, the equivalent of the whole of the North American continent, Russia is by far the largest country in the world.

Politically, modern Russia—since 1917 the Soviet Union—is all the more striking because it began only some six centuries ago with the five hundred square miles of the tiny principality of Moscow; a combination of territorial absorption and pervasive colonization has extended it from the Baltic Sea to the Pacific Coast, from the Arctic Ocean to the Black and Caspian Seas, and all along the northern borders of Persia, Afghanistan, India, and China.

But in spite of Russia's size and the wide variety of its climatic zones, from the barren tundra of the extreme north to the lush orchard groves of the Crimea and Caucasus and the cotton plantations of Turkestan, a certain monotony gives an essential unity to the Eurasian plain that stretches, undisturbed by any abrupt elevations, from Hungary to China.

The Urals, which in schoolbooks still separate Europe from Asia, are altogether negligible—a chain of dwarf hills rising no more than 1,500 feet above sea level, with any number of easy passages. There has never been any serious obstacle to movement back and forth across the great plain.

Extensive in space though Russia has been for so long, it is to European Russia that one must look for an explanation of Russian history; there, basic communications have been ensured by a ramified waterway system. The low-lying watersheds of central Russia are the sources of a number of great rivers such as the Volga, the Dnieper, and the western Dvina. Even in pre-Russian history, the cluster of great waterways formed by the outlets of the main rivers and their numerous tributaries was used by a variety of drifting peoples, who settled and came into contact with other peoples, both Western and Eastern. The waterways also promoted the conquest of Siberia, since the Volga water system merges with the western Siberian system of the Ob.

The self-centered quality of Russian history, fostered by the vastness of the Eurasian plain, was accentuated by the contrast between Russia's internal capaciousness and the relative insignificance of its shoreline. The Arctic Ocean and the White Sea are for all practical purposes useless; the Caspian Sea for all its size is landlocked. As for the Black Sea and the Baltic, they played no role in Russian history until the eighteenth century, when the cardinal traits of the nation-state were already formed.

The importance of the steppe in Russia's formation should not deflect one's attention entirely from the role of the forest belt. Though the boundary line between the forests of the north and the steppes of the south is not definite, it was the forests that shaped the Russian people in their earliest days. Going much farther south than it does now, the wooded zone started along a line passing as far south as Kiev, below present-day Moscow and Kazan. The timber zone stretched parallel to the endless steppe to its south; after dipping slightly southward along the eastern slope of the Urals to the Sayan Mountains, it resumed its eastward sweep to the Pacific Ocean. The steppe of European Russia merged imperceptibly with the steppe of

Siberian Russia, flowing through the broad passage between the Urals and the Caspian Sea.

Most of us think of Russia today as primarily agricultural because of its southern flatlands, but it was not until after the middle of the eighteenth century that the forest belts receded into the background of Russian history proper, as distinct from the history of the Asiatic invasions that influenced early Russia so profoundly via this Ural-Caspian gateway. It was, indeed, just these timberlands of north and central Russia that served the Russians as shelter whenever the steppe disgorged its burden on them. The invaders generally moved with cattle and horses, often in entire caravans; for them the forest zone was inhospitable.

The open steppe was an important factor in Russian history in a purely negative sense: not only was the steppe the natural stamping ground for the mounted Asiatic nomads, but it also served for centuries as a refuge for all sorts of malcontents in flight from the oppressive regimes that have been a permanent feature of Russian life. The southern steppe, for instance, incubated the turbulent Cossack communities.

The creation of the Russian state was thus hampered by a dual problem: on the one hand there was nothing to keep out periodic Asiatic invasions, and on the other there was no way of keeping the Russian people firmly tied to the land. The free steppe constituted a chronic leak in the state, and until the rise of modern technology and its application to the control of populations, it could not be stopped up.

Isolated individuals gradually permeated the marshy, forested hinterland in northeastern and central Russia, but the broad streams of social life could only flow along rivers and roads. The steppe was the cardinal thoroughfare; because of its far-flung, unimpeded emptiness, it was a source of disintegration both inside and out.

This emptiness was the corollary of territorial space. The country was in fact too big to be occupied by a people until they grew numerous enough, and because of the constant incursions from without this was difficult.

But—more important—the spatial vacuum was the counterpart of a cultural vacuum. Civilization came to Russia only a little more than a thousand years ago, and it came heavily mortgaged.

Civilization came with Christianity, oddly enough through the failure of Christianity elsewhere. The introduction of Christianity to Russia was a consequence of the Muslim Arab conquests of the seventh and eighth centuries. As the Muslims pushed toward the Caucasus, they thrust back a Turkic-speaking ally of Byzantium, the Khazars, into the steppe of the lower Volga and the Kuban, where the Khazars became powerful enough to maintain themselves for a couple of centuries.

Some of the Bulgar tribes whom the Khazars did not absorb emigrated north and west. One branch settled along the middle Volga, while another pushed into the lower Danube. After defeating the Byzantines, the Bulgars gradually came to dominate the whole of the eastern Balkan peninsula, adopting Slavic culture and language so thoroughly that they were to leave nothing but their name to the modern Bulgarians.

The Khazars were rather versatile for nomads; not only did they become farmers and fishermen, but they developed a great merchant empire centered on the Volga, spread out laterally between the Far East and the Black Sea and vertically between the Muslim South and the primitive forest dwellers of the North. Perhaps the Khazars' chief distinction was their conversion to Judaism, which became the official religion of the rulers and a substantial part of the population. The conversion was probably a way of fending off the Muslims on the one hand and the Byzantine Christians on the other.

The Khazars eventually were undone by the Muslim advance, and the primitive Slavs they had been patronizing found themselves adrift. It had been by way of the Khazars' pacific trading empire that the first seeds of Christianity reached the Slavs. But though Christianity acted as a cultural channel, the channel was turned into a bottleneck by the Byzantine form it took.

Through a quirk of circumstance Christianity was brought to the Slavs in their own language, not in Greek, so that the history of the Russian Church revolves around the poverty of Church Slavonic. Russian churchmen, to say nothing of their parishioners, had no need to learn Greek: the consequence was that with no Latin and no Greek, the Russians found themselves cut off on the one hand from the civilized world at large, and on the other from their own fellow-Slavs who had become Roman Catholics.

Byzantine Christianity thus had the paradoxical effect of depriving the Russians of a share of Greek civilization. While Islam avidly sponged up classical Greek thought and passed it on fruitfully to Latin Europe, and while Byzantium itself dispatched scholars and manuscripts to Italy, there was no such migration of learning to Russia.

What Russia received from Byzantium was what the court and the pious monks from Athos, Sinai, and the oriental churches could give her: a broad conception of sovereignty, in which the ruler's property was confounded with his authority;

the canon law; an art that could only be religious; an ecclesiastical education (very meager); and the habit of secluding women (which lasted for centuries). The fact that Russian clerics learned neither Greek nor Latin meant in effect that Russia missed Rome twice: the Roman Empire itself, and the Roman Catholic Church, which inherited the values of classical civilization and the pagan-Christian compound that had emerged from it. For that matter Russia also missed the Renaissance, which owed so much to the rediscovery of Greek learning.

Russian Christianity also inherited from Byzantium the profoundly rooted tradition of a detestation of the Roman Catholic world. This insulated Russia against wider cultural influences for many centuries.

All this made the Russian Church deeply and intimately national, but at the same time condemned it to a windowless chamber, the origin of the backwardness endemic in Russian life down to our own generation.

A Russian churchman once said, rightly, that "the Russian Church knows no development." Because Russian religion developed outside the Roman Catholic Church, there was no occasion for a Reformation; church and state were too densely interwoven. Nor was there the Counter-Reformation that reformed the Roman Catholic clergy and made it a potent factor in Western progress.

Finally, the closing of the seas to Russia proved decisive. Russia began with the cultural tradition of Byzantium, thinly filtered through Church Slavonic and reduced to a bagatelle in the process, but it lost even that cultural resource in the fifteenth century, when the Ottoman Turks entered the sphere of Islam and wiped out Byzantium at the very moment when Russia might have had most use for it. From the early sixteenth century on, Russia was almost closed to Roman Catholics, while Byzantium had vanished. Both Latin and Greek civilization were unavailable; Russia was cut loose in a sea of ignorance. Thus Russia's physical isolation achieved its historic significance because of the spiritual isolation that accompanied it.

Ultimately, of course, the gap between Russia and the rest of Europe was bridged, but it took so long that by the time it happened there was a yawning chasm between the upper-class recipients of European culture and the masses of the people.

By the last decades of the nineteenth century, nevertheless, the expanding educated classes swiftly reached the cultural level of Western Europe. The economy as a whole, moreover, surged forward within the free-enterprise system, with concomitant effects on the peasantry and the working class.

The autocracy itself began loosening up. In the wake of the Russian defeat in the Russo-Japanese War of 1904–5 and of a Marxist movement of agitation, the Duma, a parliamentary body with considerable powers, was set up by the Tsarist government. A constitutional monarchy seemed in the offing.

But the titanic upheavals of the First World War, which broke out in 1914, transformed Russian society. In February 1917, while Russia, alongside the Allies, was at war against the Central Powers led by Germany, the monarchy was unseated by an administrative breakdown in the capital. The Tsar's abdication was followed by eight months of "Dual Power"—a provisional government, made up of moderate upper- and middle-class elements, and the Soviet of workers' and soldiers' deputies, made up of parties led by more or less Marxist intellectuals claiming to represent the working class and peasantry.

This uneasy alliance lasted eight months: while half para-lyzed and still carrying on the war against Germany, it was ter-minated by a *putsch*: the Bolshevik branch of the Russian Social-Democratic Workers' Party established a totalitarian dictatorship that survived for generations.

CHAPTER I

THE BEGINNINGS

The mistiness of antiquity lasted much longer for Russia than for the rest of Europe. In fact nothing in any detail is known about the ancestors of the Russians until the tenth and eleventh centuries. Even the Slavs as such are not mentioned until the sixth century: before that we must be content with archeological traces of the Scythians, mentioned in the seventh century B.C. as trading with some Greek colonists north of the Black Sea.

But the Scythians vanished before the Christian era, to be succeeded by the Sarmatians, who also remain a mere name for us; they were overcome in the second and third centuries A.D. by the Teutonic Goths. It was after this that tradition began solidifying. The Goths, who spread throughout the eastern territories of the Roman Empire, were finally halted and turned back by the first of the periodic Asiatic invaders, the Huns, who expelled the Goths from the steppes north of the Black Sea and subsequently overran the Roman Empire.

The Huns were the first Asiatics to come within threatening distance of Europe as a whole. In the fifth century their leader, Attila, moved into what is today Hungary; after him came the Avars, another obscure Turkic-speaking Asiatic tribe, who appeared in the southern steppes in the second half of the sixth century.

1

The Khazars, apparently a mixture of Turkic-speakers that included Huns and Bulgars, and their allies, the Magyars (another intangible name for us), took control of the steppe north of the Black Sea by the middle of the seventh century; this is where they doubtless first came in contact with the great family of Slavic tribes, at this time still undifferentiated and all speaking much the same Indo-European language, the ancestor of the various Slavic languages of today.

The Slavs are first mentioned by Latin and Greek writers as "Sclaveni, Sclavini, Sclavi"; they split up fairly early into the great divisions that have come down to us—the southern Slavs from the Balkans, the western Slavs, including the Czechs, Moravians, and Poles, and the eastern Slavs, later known as Russians. A dimness overhangs the movements of these vanished peoples, but it may have been the collapse of the Hunnish Empire and the later invasion of the Avars that dislodged the Slavs from the Carpathian Mountains and nudged the eastern Slavs into reaching the Dnieper some time during the seventh century and then infiltrating the Russian hinterland along the great rivers.

As the Slavs gradually advanced—doubtless as a slow drift—they occupied land formerly held by the Lithuanians, who by the ninth century were gradually pushed back to a stretch of land around the Baltic Sea, in the basin of the Niemen River and the lower western Dvina. The Slavs also seem to have pushed various Finnish tribes back into the North and the East; they were to come across the Finns again later, as we shall see, when the Slavs in their turn, under the impulsion of still other ethnic drifts, began penetrating the northeastern forests. The Finns and the Lithuanians are two of the very few peoples the Slavs excelled culturally: the first contact of the Finns and Lithuanians with the outside world, which gave them the rudiments of civilization, came about because of their gradual investment by the Slavs, who in their sluggish migrations dislodged them from the great waterway that led from the Baltic to the Black and Caspian Seas.

The history of the eastern Slavs, and hence of the Russians, may be linked to this great international waterway, which led both to Byzantium and to Baghdad, and thus could serve as the spawning ground for mercantile settlements.

The Slavs had the raw products of the forest to sell: furs, honey, wax, and, above all, people. They sold both their own people and any others they could enslave. The Slav stock-in-trade consisted of the natives, who handed over both the tribute levied on them and their own persons.

The Khazar state collapsed during the tenth and eleventh centuries (it was extinguished in 1016). The Khazars succumbed to a combination of the Slavs and another Turkic-speaking people, the Patsinaks, who were instrumental in expelling the Magyars eastward. This drift had at least one important consequence: it cut off the southern Slavs from western and eastern Slavs alike. Some southern Slavs, soon after their settlement in the Balkan Peninsula, were converted to Byzantine orthodoxy. Then, when two Slavic-speaking Greek brothers from Salonika, Cyril and Methodius, were invited to Moravia in the ninth century, the formal conversion of the eastern Slavs to orthodoxy was systematized. The two Greek brothers adapted Greek capital letters to a Bulgarian dialect from Southern Macedonia, and since as late as the eleventh century the Slavonic languages were still sufficiently undifferentiated for this so-called Church Slavonic to sound to each one of them like a standardized form of itself, this dialect

3

ultimately became the language of the Russian Church and for many centuries the only literary medium available to speakers of Russian.

The collapse of the Khazar State put the politically disorganized Slavic traders in a difficult position. Finding their commerce endangered, the Slavic merchants were obliged to organize their own defense, and to do this effectively they now turned to another people, the catalyst in the crystallization of the earliest Russian state.

These were the Vikings, businessmen and bandits simultaneously. A Swedish branch of the Vikings had long before established an important international trading center in the Isle of Gothland; by the eighth century they had come by way of the Caspian Sea and Persia to sell their slaves in the markets of Baghdad.

The Vikings had already made themselves felt elsewhere; they had rowed and sailed their small ships not only across the sea but up all the main rivers of Western Europe. In the eighth century they had raided Paris and London, and had, indeed, changed the history of France and England. Then the Vikings came upon the western Dvina and the Volga in the East and saw the commercial possibilities of a waterway that led from the Baltic, at their very doorstep, to the Caspian Sea. Soon they established a trade route between Western Europe and the Muslim East.

Ultimately the Vikings found Byzantium more attractive than Baghdad, perhaps simply because it was nearer. From their point of view the Dnieper was superior to the Volga because it emptied into a real sea, and they established the great "eastern route" by way of it; Kiev thus became one of the principal stages in the Viking encirclement of Europe.

Prehistoric stone idol, from the Dolmatovo and Akulinio excavations (near Podolsk). Historical Museum, Moscow.

Russian legend—i.e., the earliest chronicles—has it that the Vikings were invited by the ancestors of the Russians to rule over them. This must be an endearingly stylized account of something far more disordered, but whether the Vikings were summoned by the Slavs to rule over them, or whether the Vikings simply conquered the Slavs and the legend was later built up out of self-regarding motives, the Vikings were employed by the Slavs along the middle Dnieper as mercenary soldiers and commission brokers.

The Russian word for Viking that has come down to us (*Varyag* or Varangian in most accounts) has always had a connotation of merchant rather than warrior. In any case the same Vikings who had produced such turmoil in Western Europe launched the Russians in their state-making. Buccaneers, adventurers, and above all merchants, the Vikings founded the Russian state. They are personified in the figure of one Rurik.

According to the chronicles, Rurik established himself in Novgorod in 862. He is in all probability the same person as a Dane of the same name who ascended the Elbe and the Rhine with a band of Norsemen, obtained sections of Friesland in fief from Emperor Lothaire (a descendant of Charlemagne), and after betraying him was expelled by the Frisians to seek his fortune elsewhere.

The Vikings were assimilated so quickly that they left no other mark. They melted into the Slavic communities they were supposed to organize. They carried on the traditional activities of the merchant princes with the same twofold aim: to maintain commerce with the East and the South, and to defend the land and the waterways from the Turkish tribes. The continuous incursions of these tribes along the great steppe and their constant harassing of the sedentary populations gave them a paramount role.

The early Russian princes were not sovereigns in any national sense—they were simply adventurers in a vast, empty, and at first foreign country. We perceive them too dimly to make a personal description either possible or interesting. Perhaps the only one worth mentioning after Rurik, the forefather of the Russian aristocracy, is Vladimir I (978–1015), a pagan who was the first specifically Russian ruler to be converted to Christianity, which he imposed on the population by force. His choice of Greek Orthodox Christianity, which he is supposed to have made after weighing the claims of Judaism and Islam, was due to his love of strong drink, prohibited by Islam, and to the ornateness of the Byzantine Church services in Constantinople as reported to him by a visitor. Aside from his conviction that the Russian joy in drinking made Christianity indispensable, his religious conversion did not interfere with his maintenance of a harem of at least eight hundred concubines.

Vladimir's conversion was an echo of Viking influence, since during their trips to Constantinople the Vikings had been impressed by the splendor of the Byzantine Church ritual (at the Saint Sophia Cathedral). In addition, some compatriots of theirs serving in the imperial bodyguard had already been converted; it was in the interests of the Byzantine Empire to convert as many barbarians as possible in order to absorb them in peace.

Accordingly, the conversion of the Russian rulers by Byzantium was a decisive factor in Russian history. Whereas the Poles and Balts were converted by missionaries originating in Germany and Sweden, the Slavic peoples of the Dnieper,

*Silver figurines, VIth century A.D., from the Martynovka treasure, near Kiev.
Historical Museum, Kiev.*

like those in the Balkans, were converted by Greek monks. The Byzantine Empire exported the religion of the Eastern Church together with its wines and brocades. The imposition of Christianity, in Russia even more than elsewhere, was accomplished by fiat from above.

It would be far-fetched to call Kievan Russia a genuine state. Not only were its boundaries uncertain, but the Slavs themselves were still partly nomadic. What the cluster of rulers descended from the legendary Rurik did was to bring together under an increasingly complicated, confused, and weakening family rule the variety of elements that populated the Russian plain. Their rule revolved around the combination of war and commerce that was the hallmark of the first few centuries of Russian history. The warfare carried on intermittently by the various Viking-Slav princelings was the source of their principal article of commerce—slaves, which is, of course, why the word for slave in most European languages is derived from the word *Slav*.

The sole objective of the Kievan princelings was the collection of tribute; the country was treated both then and later as a milchcow. The more primitive form of tribute was paid in kind, though it was also collected in the Muslim coins widely current in Russia during the Kievan period. By this time the Muslim conquests had established a great network of markets throughout the Middle East and as far afield as Khorezm in Central Asia.

Vladimir had held the title of Grand Duke of Kiev, which, since Kiev was the most important city in the region, was tantamount to acknowledging his senior authority in the Rurik clan. But the looseness of governmental relationships, as well as the sparsely settled state of the country and the continuous nomadic incursions along the ill-defined periphery of Kievan Russia, made the falling out between his sons inevitable. Vladimir's son Yaroslav was the last Grand Duke of Kiev to exercise any direct control over the whole of the realm that in theory belonged to the Rurik clan and hence to its senior member.

This whole question of imprecision in the principle of succession had its roots in the primitive concept of state authority that Rurik's descendants—the "Rurikoviches"—developed as a guide to administration. During the early period of Kievan Russia, the legal supremacy of the Grand Duke of Kiev was conceived of as an aspect of property law. Legality involved the recognition of paternal authority, plus the notion of the indivisibility of clan property. The whole area of Russia in the hands of the Rurikoviches was considered the joint property of the whole family, headed by the Grand Duke. The combination of these two notions of paternal authority and the indivisibility of property inevitably generated feuds between the princes.

Before Yaroslav died he made an attempt to circumvent this baffling principle of succession by willing his eldest son more authority than his other sons, while simultaneously partitioning the state. After his death his sons and their descendants were to consider the principalities and cities they ruled not as elements in an abstract entity known as Kievan Russia but as their personal property, and the property of their issue, to the exclusion of the other branches of the clan.

This notion of the primacy of actual property relationships symbolized the profound change taking place in the character of the formerly adventurous Vikings—they were becoming squires and administrators.

By the twelfth century the composition of Russian society was far more complicated than it had been before the advent of the Vikings, when as far as we know the people were simply divided into freemen and slaves, the slaves being the spoils of war. After the Vikings, the slaves continued to be the dregs of society: though they were normally made up of prisoners of war, anyone could become a slave by birth, bankruptcy, or voluntary agreement.

The princely clans, though the apex of society, were essentially mobile and rootless. Each prince had his own retinue, which was the source of his power: a retinue might have as many as two thousand men. By the time the princes came to number a hundred, the drain on the countryside the clan lived off must have been very substantial.

The retinue was not tied to its prince hand and foot. On the contrary, though it was customary for it to follow him about, it was not a legal duty; the custom depended on personal loyalty or egotistic interest and was prevalent before society became stratified and developed a corresponding juridical structure.

As the original Viking bands settled down, the proto-aristocracy constituted by the princely retinue began splitting up in its turn. Though a class known as *boyars*—who were to play a role in Russian life for centuries—became the most influential group, there was no clear-cut line of demarcation between them and the other free elements of society. What was to fix the aristocracy in one place as society developed was the ownership of land, which became a criterion of position as society grew more sedentary.

The boyars and other segments of the ruling groups were superimposed on the free townspeople—merchants and small artisans—and on the free peasantry. It was possible even in the earliest days for a merchant to accumulate very considerable wealth, since it was the mercantile factor that was paramount in primitive Russian society and was proportionally far better developed than crafts and farming. The international markets based on the Muslim Caliphate and the Byzantine Empire were lush enough for traders to prosper even in the basin of the remote Dnieper.

The real hallmark of the period was precisely this economic dependence not on agriculture but on the market: it was not the farming community that was politically influential during the eleventh and twelfth centuries, but the cities, based on commerce. The merchants, consequently, were far too important to be helpless vis-à-vis their princes.

The institution of the *vyeche,* or popular assembly, constituted one of the three foci of authority in Kievan Russia. It had a democratic principle, in contradistinction to the monarchical principle represented by the princes and the aristocratic principle represented by the princely retinue and its offshoots. The popular assembly spoke for the urban population. It was an effective element of government in early Russia, though neither its composition nor jurisdiction was defined with any precision.

This popular assembly was not supposed to be representative—it simply consisted of all the adult males in any given town. Decisions had to be unanimous. There was no formal way of resolving a dispute: if an agreement couldn't be reached, a free-for-all would break out and settle the question. In Novgorod, for instance, where because of the lengthy history of that city as an international trading center the popular assembly had reached the zenith of its power, brawls became tremendously violent; they would be settled on the bridge over the Volkhov River, with the losers being tossed into the freezing water.

Kiev has come down to us as the symbol of early Russian statehood, but though it was the most magnificent Russian city of the period, as well as the seat of the head of the church and the target of the incessant intrigues and feuds among the princes, it had no real foundation. In an attempt to retroject the concept of unification as far back to the beginnings of national self-consciousness as possible, Russian piety has over-emphasized the primacy of Kiev, which was never, after all, anything more than the largest center of an essentially informal federation of regional units, whose real demands were far stronger than the chimera of allegiance to a national capital.

In comparing Kievan Russia with Western Europe of the period, perhaps the most striking difference is just this root-lessness of the early rulers; that is, the absence of hierarchical social relations based on territorial attachments. Western feudalism was a rigid pyramid: everyone from the king down occupied a fixed place by birthright. A network of customs and contracts underlay the formation of classes and also welded these classes into a social organism called a state.

The hierarchical motionlessness of Western feudalism was based on a territorial theory: status depended on the connection between an individual and his *place*. The peasant was attached to his plot of land, the artisan to his guild, the bourgeois to his commune, the lord to his fief. Each one of the classes formed a sort of building block; all together made up the state.

The emptiness of Kievan Russia made this impossible. The country was too sparsely settled to be broken up into precise segments. With their economic life subject to the commerce of a great waterway, the people were accustomed to moving back and forth, looking for opportunities to trade. Without natural frontiers the armed force had to be constantly prepared to move as quickly as possible to any point that was threatened. Consequently, an individual was expected to perform the services required of him anywhere at all. In early Russia the criterion of status was thus function, not situation. This essentially horizontal character of society became even more evident when the roving, fluid Kievan society was overlaid centuries later by the evolving Moscow state, rooted firmly in land relationships.

For the first few centuries, to be sure, the conversion of Russia to Christianity was nominal: very often the higher clergy—to say nothing of the lower—knew nothing about Christian dogma at all. The primitive Slavs retained an essentially magical interest in their religion, which was facilitated by the unintelligibility of the Church Slavonic that was its medium. Linguistically, of course, it might have been considered a standard form of the local speech, but no one actually understood it, not even the scattering of educated people. It was perhaps just this obscure and unintelligible ritual, as well as the flowing robes and sacred vestments of the clergy, plus the threat of eternal damnation, that gave the church its prestige.

The Kievan period is generally thought to have ended in 1169, when Andrew Bogolyubsky, the son of Yuri Dolgoruki, Prince of Rostov and Suzdal, stormed Kiev and pulverized it. This was the first time a Russian prince had given Kiev the treatment reserved for non-Russian cities. Kiev was plundered and sacked, churches and monasteries were burned, and the people slaughtered, expelled, and enslaved. The sack of Kiev represents the triumph of the disruptive forces in early Russia, which the competition of the grand dukes, unbridled by any constitutional regime, had sorely aggravated.

From the beginning of the eleventh century on, the sufferings of the Kievan Russians made them turn to an expedient that has been a leitmotif of Russian history—they took to their heels. There was no sudden exodus, but very gradually a migration began that cut into the population along the Dnieper. Rich and poor began drifting westward and northward to elude the immediate prospect of being robbed, raped, slaughtered, or enslaved.

The stream of migration along what was called the "straight road" from Kiev to the Volga—along a Dnieper tributary, the Desna—ultimately led to the establishment of Moscow. It was another example of the characteristic phenomenon of Russian colonization via a river; the banks of the Desna, passing through dense thickets infested by robbers, were quite underpopulated.

After Kiev's political submergence, its western neighbors, Galicia and Volynia, grew in importance, only to find themselves outflanked by two different movements. First the Mongols appeared; I shall speak of them in a moment. Then, in the marshy forested region of the Niemen Basin, the Lithuanians, an ancient race still pagan, who had withstood the movement of proselytization launched by the German military monks, suddenly and surprisingly claimed the attention of history by embarking on a program of conquest under some able rulers. They extended their power to the Dnieper, turned Kiev into a Lithuanian city, and subjected Western Russia to Vilna, their capital. Greek Orthodox Christians found themselves in thrall to pagans in the west just as they were being politically effaced by Mongols in the east.

By the beginning of the fifteenth century, the Grand Duchy of Lithuania embraced a large area, including the basin of the upper and the middle-western Dvina, the Niemen, the southern Bug, the Dnieper, and the upper Oka.

Because of all this, what was to become the Russian state began to form only when Muscovy emerged during the thirteenth and fourteenth centuries.

Kiev's place was taken at first not by Moscow, which, first mentioned in 1147, was wholly negligible in the twelfth century, but by Vladimir, in the Principality of Rostov-Suzdal, not far from Moscow. Vladimir was taken by Andrew Bogolyubsky after he ravaged Kiev. In Vladimir, Andrew could do as he pleased. He would have had more trouble in Rostov and Suzdal, which were older than Vladimir, with relatively independent boyars and popular assemblies.

The forests, immune to the caravans and hordes of the nomads, gave the fleeing Russians a natural shelter, and since Russian peasants were pacific by nature and the Finns even more so, the Finns met by the Russian farmers in the forests of the northeast completely accepted them and intermingled with them. It was a typical frontier situation. The topography of northeastern Russia militated against the creation of large villages such as those common in southern Russia; the country was covered by virgin timber and marshes that were difficult to cultivate.

As for the princes, they too changed swiftly in response to the contrast between this environment and Kievan Russia. The new combination engendered a different social structure. The northeastern princes became similar to the American pioneers who went west to carve their own estates out of the new lands. Contemplating the land they had laid their hands on, they regarded it as personal property, theirs by virtue of their own toil and sweat and disposable as they saw fit.

The boyars themselves began turning into a squirearchy, since the established tradition of princely rewards for services now took the form of land-grants. This practice broke up the territory into innumerable tiny principalities, and thus, by accentuating the fragmentation of the region, enabled the future Moscow dynasty to impose on the atomized principalities a degree of centralization that has characterized Russian affairs ever since.

The atomization of northeastern Russia, combined as it was with the principle of allocating land to the boyars in the service of some particular prince, led to a clash of interests between princes and boyars. The boyars were bound to be hostile to any change in their rulers. A change meant that a new prince, accompanied by new boyars, would be coming along to oust them. The selfish interests of the boyars tended to make them support their prince's dynastic ambitions insofar as these princes were determined to maintain the local dynasty. But since the princes had inherited the tradition of looking on the principality they ruled as a piece of family real estate, and since they tended to divide the land among their heirs, they not only collided with the economic interest of the boyars, but they constantly generated clan warfare, which exasperated the boyars, who by now had their roots in the soil. We shall see how the interplay of these factors led to the emergence of the Russian autocracy some centuries later.

The boyar aristocracy was an element of stability; it was the boyars' interest to establish order, which at that time could be accomplished only by the emergence of a strong house, in this case the Grand Duchy of Vladimir.

To sum up the period politically, the main tendency was a growth in the strength of both princes and boyars, with consequent collisions, while the popular assemblies declined rapidly. This process, so full of meaning for all subsequent Russian history, throughout which we see the chasm widening between the summits of society and the people, was consummated on the eve of the Mongol invasion.

Russia was pulverized by ferocious strife. The princes detested each other and were incapable of cooperating with the boyar aristocracy they depended on. Also, the decline of the popular assembly reflected the growing oppression of the rural population as well as the growth of the landed estates of the boyars and princes. Rural Russia had in fact been launched on the course that was to lead to bondage.

But peace was about to be forced on the country for a time by the last of the Asiatic invaders, and the ablest—the Mongols.

CHAPTER II

THE MONGOLS

With the advent of the Mongols, who became known to the Russians and thence to the world as Tatars, Russian history encounters a factor qualitatively unique.

For the Mongols, who exacted tribute from the Russians for 240 years, we must change our perspective. There is no point looking at the Mongols through Russian eyes; the Russians must be seen through Mongol eyes. From the Mongol point of view, the Russian adventure was simply an episode, on the whole a minor one, in a campaign of conquest that included China and Central Asia; the campaign failed in Russia not through Russian action but because the Mongol realm began to decompose from within.

Around 1300, the Mongol Empire extended from China to Poland, occupying the whole of Asia except India, Burma, and Cambodia. When we consider that the Mongol people numbered possibly a million, while the peoples they controlled amounted to some 100 million, and that at their zenith the Mongols had fewer than 150,000 troops, it is obvious that the leadership of this small group of nomads was based on something special.

Russian history between the thirteenth and fifteenth centuries is incomprehensible without the Mongol background. Fundamental decisions were made by the Great Khan of the

Mongols, who held his residence in Mongolia or in China. This meant that the Russian vassals of the Khan of the Golden Horde—the Mongol unit encamped in Russia—were really governed by the ruler of Peking. The structure and function of the Golden Horde itself, and hence of Russia, was established by the founder of the Mongol Empire, Chingis Khan, whose followers considered him enjoined by heaven to rule the world.

Conversely, Russia made a substantial contribution to the power both of the Golden Horde and of the Mongol Empire it was part of. Russians drafted into the Mongol armies played an important role in the campaigns of the Khans of the Golden Horde as well as of the Great Khans themselves. Russia was milked for craftsmen and artisans of all kinds, who worked both in the Golden Horde and as far east as Mongolia.

In short, though Russian historians have generally had a biased view of Mongol influence, either pretending it was on the whole negligible, or on the contrary magnifying its negative effects and blaming the Mongols for Russian backwardness, their bias cannot obscure the fact that Russian political life was molded by Mongol politics for two centuries and more.

The Mongols were unknown in Europe and the Middle East before their sudden appearance in the thirteenth century. They were the last of the long line of invaders of the western steppe—the proto-Persians (Scythians and Sarmatians), and the Turkic-speaking Huns, Avars, Khazars, Patsinaks, and Cumans. The interaction between Turks and Mongols was always intimate; a substantial portion of the Mongol armies were Turks under Mongol officers.

The Mongols had an extraordinarily efficient striking force based on a swift coordination of light and heavy cavalry that was far superior to anything else at the time. It was not, to be

The mosaic-decorated interior of Saint Sophia, of Kiev, one of the finest examples of Byzantine art in Russia, and of Kievan Russian civilization. The building of this church was started under Yaroslav the Wise in 1037. At the top of the curved apse, against a gold background, stands the isolated, colossal figure of the Virgin. Below, the Communion of the Apostles, with Christ shown twice, on the right and the left of the ciborium, each Christ offering bread and wine to six Apostles.

21

sure, an innovation, but rather the perfecting of the traditional mounted steppe warfare. The horses, like their riders, had immense stamina. The Mongol light cavalry was armed with bow and arrow; their heavy cavalry carried sabre, lance, a battleaxe or mace, and a lasso, with a helmet of leather (later of iron) and a leather cuirass or coat of mail.

But perhaps the most effective thing about the Mongol armies was their strategy: they succeeded by applying the principles of a hunt—the Great Battue—that they held every year at the beginning of the winter. It was a basic rite in the training of adult warriors. During the Great Battue, hunters would be deployed around an area comprising thousands of square miles. There was a center and a right and left wing, each with its special commander. After the columns had been deployed, the Great Khan himself, together with his concubines and his commissariat, set up camp in the center of the Battue. The lines would then gradually converge—it took from one to three months—and drive the game into the presence of the Great Khan. Couriers kept the Khan informed of the location and quantity of the game. If any of the game slipped out through a badly manned section of the ring, the commanding officer would be personally liable to severe penalties.

After the game had been driven into a circle about ten miles in circumference, which would be marked off by lines of ropes, the ring was sealed. While huge numbers of panicky animals milled about inside, the Great Khan would go inside the inner ring and begin the shooting, followed in turn by princes of the blood, army commanders, and then ordinary soldiers, all slaughtering the animals for a number of days.

Now, when the Mongols were about to launch a military campaign, the Great Council would convene as a staff headquarters. Operations and targets would be laid down, with the captains of all the major army units present to be given their orders. Special agents had already been sent to spy on the land to be attacked; as much information as possible about the people and the countryside was collected in advance. The marshalling grounds and take-off area for the army were designated, and appropriate pasturing grounds were reserved along the route to be taken by the troops.

This procedure was not a mere matter of information gathering; secret agents, sent out long before the troops were to start marching, carried on systematic propaganda and psychological warfare. The Mongol approach was to persuade the religious minorities that the Mongols tolerated all religions, the poor that the Mongols would be against the rich—and for that matter they actually were against the rich, i.e., the enemy rich—and the merchants that the Mongol peace would make the routes safe for business. Everyone was promised safety if he surrendered and frightful vengeance if he did not.

The Mongols believed in war *à outrance*—their goal was the physical extirpation of their opponents' armies. This was where the Great Battue came in. The Mongols would first envelop a vast area and then tighten the ring around it. The columns operated with astonishing coordination, communication between them being kept up by couriers or smoke signals. If by some chance the enemy was too strong at first for the Mongols to burst through his lines, they would pretend to retreat; as a rule the enemy would then break ranks and rush forward in hot pursuit, thinking the Mongols had been routed. The Mongols then would pivot quickly on their agile little horses, reform their ring, and this time finish things off.

The Presentation in the Temple. Bronze panel from the doors of Saint Sophia of Novgorod. Each door has thirteen panels. There were originally three doors, only two are left.

Because the army was supposed to live off the conquered area and was followed by a camel caravan with only a minimum of supplies, the Mongol strategy worked on the assumption that the seizure of huge enemy territories was not only feasible, but lucrative: thus, the smaller the Mongol armies the better. The Mongol army kept growing as it advanced through enemy territory by levies made on the native population. The peasants would be drafted to besiege fortresses and drive carts, while urban craftsmen were drafted into the engineering corps or manufacturing units to make weapons and tools. The Mongol army would often be stronger at the end of a campaign than at the beginning. When Chingis died the Mongol army proper numbered only 129,000, probably its zenith.

All this of course sounds strikingly modern—both the practice of living off the land and the principle of extreme mobility in warfare. Consequently, though military historians traditionally have disregarded Mongol strategy and tactics, interest in them has now revived, precisely in the era of tanks and airplanes: the fast, far-flung Mongol columns of horsemen are startlingly reminiscent of the most effective techniques of the Second World War.

The helplessness of the Russian princes is amply demonstrated by the nine voyages to Saray made by Ivan I of Moscow (1325–1341), and the five made by his son Simeon (1341–1353). The granting of the executive license, which took the form of a ceremony of enthronement, was carried out in the name of the Khan and in the presence of his ambassador: it was a dramatic illustration of the peremptory nature of Mongol rule. All in all, between 1242 and 1430, some 130 Russian princes journeyed to the Khans and to the Great Khans, sometimes for purely personal objectives.

The interests of the Mongol rulers were simple: they wanted revenue and recruits, the basic requirements of their Empire. The Russian princes became tax collectors; by the fourteenth century they had replaced the Mongol officials who, supported by a police force, had originally been posted in charge of taxation all over the country.

The Russians cooperated closely with the Tatars even in the earliest times. Not only did the Russians take part in the military adventures of their conquerors, as indicated above, but the Tatars gave the Russian princes great support in the struggle against their enemies on Russia's southern and western borders. The symbiosis between Tatars and Russians was very close.

One of the oldest examples of state regalia in the Kremlin's State Armory Museum, Moscow, is this fur-trimmed Monomachos Cap of State. The top is in curving gold filigree against a flat gold ground, studded with cabuchon jewels and pearls. It is said to have belonged to Vladimir Monomakh, the Kievan leader who attempted to establish a centralized state, but Vladimir died over a hundred years before this cap was made.

Economically, the Golden Horde itself was a symbiosis between nomadic and sedentary population. The Tatars found pasturage for their cattle and horses in the steppes of southern Russia and the northern Caucasus, while the edges of the steppe were also used for crops.

In addition, the Tatars had a great interest in commerce, which was aided by the location of Saray on the lower Volga. This was the ancient trade route to the east, which enabled the Tatars to create a system of commercial exchange points between east and west. These commercial settlements stimulated exchange between merchants from many countries, and the Tatars themselves played a part in it, contributing horses, hides, and leather goods.

The Russo-Tatar symbiosis was particularly intense at the summit of Russian society, that is, the princes and boyars, who often married Tatar princesses. Oddly enough, Tatar influence in Russian domestic affairs began to increase *after* the decline of the Golden Horde, which began about the middle of the fourteenth century and culminated in the collapse of the Tatar state a century later. After this collapse, numerous detachments of Tatar princes and high functionaries poured into Russia, accompanied by throngs of servants and armed troops. As Moscow began to ascend, it attracted them into service; it could offer them more than could the crumbling Golden Horde.

By the end of the seventeenth century, the Moscow upper class is estimated to have been about 17 percent Tatar or oriental. But the Tatar influence was far more than a question of bloodliness: the state that evolved during the sixteenth century and lasted some 400 years was an offshoot of the monolithic rule of the Tatars. The Tatars, once feared, then mingled with and imitated, were the prototype of the Tsarist autocracy. They had reduced the relatively independent squirearchy to subservience, first to the Grand Dukes of Moscow and later to the Tsars. The popular assembly, which had been declining rapidly even before the Tatars' appearance, lost its most important function under the Golden Horde—the right it once had to choose and oust its princes. The Khans took over this prerogative. The popular assembly vanished, leaving the bulk of the people to sink still further under the twofold burden of domestic and Tatar exactions.

Combat between Russians and Tatars in 1238. XVIth century miniature from the Historical Museum, Moscow. The Mongolian invasion, women and cattle included, swept across the Siberian steppe in 1237; their power was to last two and a half centuries.

The Tatar experiment in dominion, in spite of its immense initial success, finally failed. Perhaps this was because the technology of the time made it impossible to maintain a centralized empire spread so thin over such a vast territory. It represents a curious embryonic parallel to the still more brilliant nomadic attempt to rule a sedentary civilization that was embodied in the Slave Household of the Ottoman Empire during the period of its efflorescence (roughly 1365–1565).

Nomads in general all face the same problem with respect to the sedentary peoples they have overrun: unless they want to give up their nomadic ways and settle down themselves, intermingling with their subjects and sooner or later vanishing, they must apply to men the methods that have been successful with their flocks and herds: they become shepherds of men. What the Tatars did (though only partially, as we can see by the far more extensive system of their Ottoman cousins) was to use the Russian princes to ride herd. This failed eventually because the fabric of Russian life was not transformed or even changed substantially, so that when the Tatar Empire began to crumble under its own internal tensions, Russian society was still vigorous enough to take advantage of this enfeeblement of Tatar authority and resume its autonomous evolution.

The Russians thought the Tatars glamorous. Though one side of Russian secular literature expressed a conventional feeling of hatred for the national oppressor, and the heroic folk-sagas recording the conflict with the previous enemy, the Cumans, were recast to fit the Tatars, a contrary fascination also rooted itself in literature. It has, indeed, remained a permanent motif in Russian literature to this day. Tatar chivalry in warfare was much admired, as was the life of the steppe, with its free nomadic ways, which during the nineteenth century were very attractive to Russian writers.

In the fifteenth century the Tatar-Russian union in the upper classes was so intimate that the court of Basil II of Moscow actually spoke Turkish, the general language of the Golden Horde. Indeed, many Russian noblemen in the fifteenth, sixteenth, and seventeenth centuries even adopted Tatar surnames, perhaps the best known examples being the Velyaminovs, of Viking ancestry, who took the Turkish name of Aksakov. A descendant of the Tatars was to become a famous propagandist for the Slavophile viewpoint of the nineteenth century, and the philosopher Shaadayev, a zealous pro-Westerner, was a descendant of Chingis' son Chagatay. Many well-known Russian families are of Tatar descent, including the Yusupovs, Kutuzovs, and Urusovs. The Tatars even produced a Russian Tsar, Boris Godunov.

CHAPTER III

THE RISE OF THE MOSCOW STATE: IVAN THE TERRIBLE

In some ways Russian feudalism resembled that of Western Europe. Government was still only feebly centralized; there were great estates and a hierarchy among landlords; the landlords were delegated judicial and fiscal powers; the reciprocal services of boyars and tenants were governed by contract. But the principle paramount in Western Europe—hereditary relationships and their objective, i.e., impersonal, foundation—was generally absent.

Feudalism never crystallized as it did in Europe. Aside from the fact that the Russian princes did not embody different dynastic claims, as did the great feudal houses in France and Germany, the people themselves had no regional characteristics. The Russian nationality was formed long before the Russian nation-state. This was partly due to the abovementioned social fluidity. Also, property symbolized nothing. A principality, in accordance with the ancient Viking attitude, was simply a piece of real estate. At bottom this notion is profoundly antifeudal. The wills left by Suzdalian and Muscovite princes treated cities, villages, jewels, and furs on exactly the same level. Russian feudalism was thus essentially different from Western European feudalism—contracts were absolutely revocable: this was primarily because relations were not between things, but between people.

There was no question of "great vassals" as in France. Russia was divided up between the members of what was theoretically a single family who were all equal in terms of lineage and might go up or down in life in accordance with nothing but their luck. This also applied to the lords owning their land outright: whether they were descendants of the old princely retinues, or favorites of the moment, or people performing services for a prince and rewarded by land, their material and spiritual status was a function of a contract they had concluded with him. As far as the prince was concerned, what they had was not a title of nobility but a function.

Consequently, there was not even a clear line between plebeians and nobility. The basest villein could be elevated by receiving a charter of immunity from a prince, as could a boyar or the head of a convent.

In a word, the whole complex of relations revolving around the notions of privilege, status, and immunity was based on an economic, not a political, concept. Thus all functionaries of the state, however exalted, were mere employees who could be sacked at will.

Hence, chivalry was an alien idea. The success of the Roman Catholic Church in moralizing combat by creating the concept of the knight "without fear and without reproach" had no counterpart in the Russian Church, which was indifferent to the organization of society. Everything in Western Europe to do with honor, whether of the class, family, or individual—chivalric orders, duels, tournaments, heraldry—was completely absent in Russia.

When boyars and princes spoke of "honor," what they meant was a rank they claimed in a genealogical hierarchy; it involved no duties. The extraordinary unscrupulousness of the society thus was unbridled even by lip service: neither lying, perjury, nor assassination was regarded as something beneath a prince's dignity. Deceit was not only commonplace, but admired; treachery aimed at securing a brother's or cousin's death was quite acceptable. In this as in other things the customs of Russia seem an echo of a more ancient past, of France, for instance, under the Merovingians and Carolingians, before the rise of a moral ethos humanized manners.

Russia missed the Middle Ages, just as it missed the influence of Rome and the Renaissance. If the Middle Ages are taken to span the end of Roman civilization and the beginning of the Renaissance, then Russia, unacquainted with either one, simply remained unarticulated throughout this period. It remained submerged in the religious conception of individual and social life until the reign of Peter the Great and, if the masses of the people are kept in mind, for generations afterwards.

At the very beginning of Russian society the original ownership of land had doubtless derived from occupation or purchase. Land acquired in this way was the absolute property of the owner, whose only obligation to the authorities was paying taxes. A landowner might be granted all sorts of exemptions and privileges by the prince controlling his land, such as the right to act as judge over those living on it. He might also be designated tax collector for the prince; also, the estate, for one reason or another, might be exempt from taxation altogether. These privileges were all defined in some detail in actual letters patent issued by the prince to a landowner; it was the lands held in outright possession under such conditions that were known as patrimonial or hereditary estates.

Saint George and the Dragon. Georgian enamel, XVth century. Tiflis Museum.

34

The patrimonial domain was distinct from another source of land ownership—service tenure—that became widespread during the thirteenth and fourteenth centuries, when the problem afflicting the country as a whole was still the scarcity of manpower. Land was very abundant, but without development it meant nothing. The princes' revenues would be magnified immensely if waste or fallow lands were converted into agricultural settlements, which they might secure by granting individuals and monasteries estates, and they did so.

The upper class grew more stratified. The boyars, who owned land that they exploited with servile or semi-servile labor, depended for their economic independence on the size of their estates, though their independence as individuals still benefited by the custom inherited from the ancient retinues of the Viking princes and their successors, according to which they were under no obligation to serve their prince simply because they lived or held land within his political sphere. This privilege was always paid lip service to in agreements between boyars and princes; since this was the only guarantee of the landed aristocracy's independence, it was highly cherished. Boyars never showed the slightest hesitation in changing sides at their convenience, nor was there ever any legal impediment to this. The princes were in no position to challenge this privilege since they were often weak and found the boyars indispensable; for that matter the custom often worked in their favor.

This gradual imposition on the population of the duty of service was even more important in the case of the farmers, who had formerly been free and were now gradually slipping into a network of obligations to the owner of the land they worked as well as to the state. Though the process in its early phases is obscure, it seems that the formerly independent farmers eventually became tenants on land owned variously by princes, boyars, or the Church. In some cases big landlords, both secular and ecclesiastical, would simply seize land belonging to weaker neighbors, but more generally the privileges the princes could bestow on estates both of boyars and of the church, especially in taxation, were a great inducement for the farmer to exchange his nominal independence for the protection of a powerful lord. This inducement grew during the Tatar occupation; since both before and after this landlords had a vital interest in manpower, the farmer might well come to think it better to have a protector interposed between himself and the voracious treasury official.

In any case, by the fourteenth century tenant farming seems to have been far more common than independent small farming. Slavery had meanwhile become a negligible factor, especially since prisoners of war, its chief source, had vanished with the pacification of the national territory.

Relations between tenants and landlords and between princes and boyars evolved in the same direction. At first the tenant could theoretically leave his landlord and work for whomever he pleased whenever his contract had expired, while the landlord, contrariwise, could also dismiss his tenants. But the tenant's right to go wherever he wished was soon encroached on. The prince had a fundamental interest in keeping his taxpaying population within his reach, and the farmers' freedom of movement began to be hampered, initially through agreements made by the Grand Dukes of Moscow with the other princes binding each other not to accept free peasants leaving each other's domains.

At first such restrictions did not touch the actual freedom of the tenant; they merely increased the difficulty of finding a new landlord by limiting the freedom of the landlords themselves in this respect. But this was only the first step; a further restriction, applied by the middle of the fifteenth century, made it impossible for the tenant to leave whenever he chose during the year, which had formerly been his right, and restricted him to the fortnight preceding and following St. George's Day (26 November). This restriction was the beginning of a trend.

Against this complex background the Moscow dynasty emerged, a powerful centralizing and state-making factor that in the space of a few generations began playing a positive role abroad as well as at home. The components of the new Moscow state were not themselves new—if only to judge by their churches, Rostov, Suzdal, and Vladimir had a substantial history behind them—but in fact the collapse of Kiev turned out to have marked the end of an epoch, the rise of Moscow the beginning.

Moscow was the focus of three groups of water-routes: the western group to Northern Europe via the Baltic; the Volga-Middle East route it acquired in 1552–56; and the north-eastern route to Siberia, where the precious furs came from that have always produced so much foreign revenue for Russia. The first two routes, which were a basic transit route from northern Europe to Persia, connected Moscow with the world market; Moscow became firmly embedded in the rapidly developing commercial revolution then sweeping Europe as a whole, especially after the English discovered the White Sea route to Russia in 1553.

Moscow focused all the forces hostile to the permanent dismemberment of the country: its chief rival at the time, Tver, was preoccupied by complex affairs in the west, while Moscow's interests were simultaneously more comprehensive and because of its central position more "national." In the west Moscow's interests took in Novgorod, Tver, Lithuania, and the Baltic countries; in the south and east, the Golden Horde; and, as a permanent accompaniment to all this, the currents of colonization and commerce along the Volga.

As a great landowner, the Church shared these material preoccupations of the landed aristocracy; at the same time it had the further goal, as heir to the Byzantine claims to universality, of having one Russian metropolitan (or bishop) as the sole head of the Church. This naturally made the Church a strong supporter of union as against princely strife.

Russia unification may be summed up as the consequence of two interwoven processes: the unification of the Principality of Moscow under its "senior" Princes, their fusion with the Grand Dukes of Vladimir, and the establishment as a result of the "Grand Duchy of Moscow, of Vladimir, and all Russia"—the forerunner of the Muscovite Tsardom.

Both Muscovy and America were discovered by Western Europe at about the same time. With the growth of Muscovy, it gradually became evident that Europe did not end, as had been thought, on the northeastern frontier of Lithuania and Poland.

The increasing importance of Muscovy led to a momentous development in the Russian Church. When Moscow became a sovereign state in 1480, in the wake of the Golden Horde's dissolution, it grew into a situation in which it found itself the only independent Greek Orthodox community. Byzantium had been conquered and suppressed by the Ottoman Turks in 1453, only five years after Russia had acquired the right to elect and consecrate her own metropolitans as a by-product of the council of Roman Catholic and Greek Orthodox dignitaries that had met in Ferrara and Florence in 1438 to bridge the great schism.

The Russian Church no longer could look to Byzantium on the one hand or the Tatars on the other to protect it against the growing power of the Grand Dukes. Weak, primitive, utterly unlettered, the Church not only tacitly submitted to the primacy of the grand ducal power but actively promoted the expansion of Muscovy by expounding a theory of allegiance that made of Moscow a "third Rome."

This theory was engagingly simple: since the first Rome had fallen because it had betrayed true (i.e., Greek Orthodox) Christianity, and Constantinople, the second Rome, had been taken by the infidel for the same reason, Moscow was the natural heir of these two other backsliding Romes and would, moreover, continue forever. This theory was actually an adaptation of earlier theories commonly held in other Slavic and Balkan countries, especially Bulgaria, but it lacked the element of a definite material link between Constantinople and Moscow. Logic required some factual support to enable Ivan III and Basil III to assume the mantle of Byzantium.

Ivan III had married Sophïe Paleologue, niece of the last Byzantine emperor, who had been killed by the Turks when they took Constantinople. The fact of this marriage was now supplemented by a brilliant lyrical invention that made the Moscow house not only the direct descendant of a so-called Pruss, supposed to be a brother of Caesar Augustus, but also traced the transmission of Christianity not to Byzantium but directly back to Andrew, a (putative) brother of the Apostle Peter.

With these additions, the old theory was enough to give the Moscow Grand Dukes the most splendid genealogy imaginable and make them leaders of Greek Orthodoxy in their own right. This theoretical cornerstone of the growing Muscovite absolutism was then reinforced by some further apologetics buttressing the alliance between the Church and the State by stating that blind, obedient faith was the only road to salvation and proscribing the use of reason altogether. The slightest show of independent thought was heresy and blasphemy *per se*; the only acceptable arguments were scriptural quotations.

The concentration of power in the Muscovite autocracy changed life in Moscow and at court. The new status of the crown had to be made manifest by the embellishment of the city; both Ivan III and Basil III exerted themselves to do this. Italian architects were imported for the building of cathedrals and churches; the palaces of the Grand Dukes were built of stone, instead of the wood that had been used in the much less pretentious houses they had been living in; the Kremlin was given a ring of stone walls and towers. The court developed an elaborate ceremonial, possibly under the influence of Sophie Paleologue. Ivan III, who often used the title of "Sovereign of all Russia by the Grace of God," was occasionally also referred to as "Tsar and Autocrat," thought the Russian connotation of this was simply that he was independent of the Tatars. The unification of the realm was symbolized by the adoption of the two-headed eagle of Byzantium.

The development of a strong centralized monarchy at the time was not at all peculiar to Russia. Ivan III (1462–1505) was contemporary with the English War of the Roses and the rise of the Tudor dynasty; strong monarchies were pushing forward in other countries in Europe.

But the growth of the Muscovite autocracy far outstripped the parallel development of monarchy elsewhere in Europe. In 1517, when an envoy from the Holy Roman Empire (the Austrian Baron Sigismund von Herberstein) visited Moscow, he felt as though he were entering an entirely different political atmosphere, and that Basil III had completely outdone any other monarch in the degree of his power over his subjects.

It was during the reign of Ivan the Terrible, the longest in Russian history (1533–1584), that the autocracy was streamlined and formulated.

Ivan the Terrible; Italian engraving.

The cathedral of Saint Basil on Red Square, Moscow, built by Ivan the Terrible to commemorate his victories over the Tatars between 1554 and 1560. The Russian architects used traditional forms of wood construction and added eight cupolas, all different, and a central pyramid. The exuberant variety of the exterior is made even more exotic by multi-colored decoration of tiles and paint.

Ivan was the first to rule Russia as a wholly autocratic Tsar in theory as well as in practice. Three years old at the death of his father Basil III, he grew up in a period when the savagery of the princely and boyar cliques and clans kept lapsing into the violence that, while largely repressed under the thumb of Basil III, had kept breaking out under the regency of Ivan's mother. Deportations, confiscations of estates, tortures, assassinations, and executions were commonplace.

Ivan's nickname seems well deserved, though in Russian it properly denotes menace and has sometimes been translated as "Dread." He became known for an extreme kind of sadism while still a boy, and grew up with a combination of extreme piety of the Russian type—obsessive devotion to the external observances of the Church and utter indifference to the inner meaning of the religion, to say nothing of its ethics—and extravagant sexual license.

He had himself crowned "Tsar of all the Russias" at the age of seventeen and thus made official a title that had been used only casually during the preceding century. The word had meant nothing characteristic beforehand: it was also used to refer to the Khan of the Golden Horde.

Ivan seems to have been a paranoiac. His mistrustfulness made him kill almost anyone who came into contact with him. Executions by him were commonplace on all levels of society, generally accompanied by the most ingeniously contrived tortures. After 1560 especially, when Ivan decided he had been a mere tool of his counselors during his early days, he conducted a wholesale massacre among members of his family, Church dignitaries, princes, boyars, and commoners.

During an expedition Ivan undertook against Novgorod in 1570 to punish it for remissness, churches were desecrated, pillaged, and burnt; priests were flogged, tortured and executed in public. But it was rare for Ivan to miss mass; he spent a great deal of his time composing monastic rules or contriving complicated ceremonies for the consecration of the metropolitan. This did not stop him from treating his metropolitans with the utmost ferocity. An archbishop of Novgorod is said to have been sewn into a bear's skin and thrown to the dogs.

Ivan's prey generally met their deaths in churches, quite often during the mass. In the midst of the most extravagant bloodbaths, Ivan kept lists of the people he had murdered; he distributed money to monasteries to pay for the victims' eternal repose. Some 4,000 names of those killed were listed; the true number is thought to have been much larger. Obsessed, doubtless rightly, by terror of plots and general catastrophe, he wrote Queen Elizabeth in 1569 asking for asylum should he be ejected from Russia. He offered to make the arrangement reciprocal; she declined.

Ivan's rule may be summed up as the elevation of state authority to institutional as well as practical supremacy. To some extent this involved the apparent magnification of local authorities, since Ivan curtailed the highhandedness of some of the provincial governors still battening off the local populations. Socially, Ivan's contribution to the centralization of state authority took the form of destroying the power of the landed aristocracy, whom his wrath, generally quite indiscriminate in its choice of targets, eventually fixed on and blighted.

Aside from these long-range sociological innovations, Ivan's reign was marked by the decisive beginning of the protracted eastward expansion of the Russian state. Strife between the Tatar states of Kazan and Astrakhan on the Volga enabled Ivan to conquer and annex them both, Kazan in 1552 and Astrakhan in 1556. This eastward movement led to the absorption of western Siberia, which was carried on by purely private initiative as a result of the trading operations of the Stroganov family, which had been assigned large estates near the Urals and given permission to extract metals and salt and to extend its domain beyond the mountains. The Stroganovs had a private army, formed of Cossacks and the haphazard bands of Lithuanian and Muscovite fugitives who roamed the southern Russian steppe. One of these Cossacks, Yermak, who was under sentence of death for rebellion, led about one hundred fifty freebooters into Siberia in September 1581. By 1582 he had a hold on two great Siberian rivers, the Irtysh and the Obi. In return for a full pardon and a few presents, he handed over his conquests to the Moscow crown. This marked the beginning of the long Russian advance to the Pacific Ocean, which was reached by 1643, mainly through a process of permeation, with very few armed conflicts and scarcely any government help at all.

The ruthless concentration of authority in the Moscow state, consummated during the reign of Ivan the Terrible, plus the disastrous evolution of socio-economic conditions throughout the rapidly growing country, soon led to an extraordinary upheaval, which, though prepared for over many decades, was launched by a dynastic crisis.

In 1581, Ivan, in a fit of rage, killed his son and heir, personally, with a metal-tipped staff he used to carry; the young man had apparently been trying to shield his pregnant wife against his father's brutality. Ivan spent a good deal of time repenting, but when he died in 1584—characteristically after taking monastic vows on his death-bed—the only heir to the throne was his remaining feebleminded son, Theodore, who died in 1598. His death extinguished the Muscovite dynasty and led directly to the "Time of Troubles."

CHAPTER IV

PETER THE GREAT

The years that followed Ivan's death were full of ungovernable turbulence. Since Ivan's successor, Tsar Theodore, was feebleminded (wholly concentrated on the ringing of church bells), his brother-in-law, Boris Godunov, who had been a favorite of Ivan the Terrible's, took advantage of his sister's influence over the sickly Tsar and made himself the *de facto* ruler of the country. Boris was thus the temporary victor in the dense swarm of palace intrigues and internecine boyar conflicts that had broken out upon Ivan the Terrible's death.

Godunov established himself so thoroughly that, on Tsar Theodore's death without issue, he easily arranged to have himself elected Tsar by a so-called Territorial Assembly; the election did no more than inflame the old intrigues all over again. Godunov, formerly considered charming and amiable, soon lost his appeal. The upper classes found themselves in much the same situation as under Ivan the Terrible, with deportations, confiscations, and executions everyday events.

All this was climaxed by a great famine that lasted from 1601 to 1603. Both merchants and landlords became profiteers; confiscations were accompanied by the release of slaves, who were forbidden to find another master, while many other slaves were merely turned out to forage for themselves. Banditry grew rife; the flood of peasants already drifting away from the encroachments of serfdom was increased by a torrent of famished and dislocated refugees.

The general disaffection crystallized in the False Dmitri, a pretender to the throne—the first of many—who with the assistance of the Polish government led a movement against Godunov. Dmitri claimed to be a son of Ivan the Terrible, who in his account was supposed to have died in 1591 under enigmatic circumstances. Dmitri's actual identity seems irremediably obscure. In any case, in 1603 the False Dmitri took up headquarters with Mniszek, an adventurous Polish nobleman. Dmitri had numerous Polish connections—he even married his host's daughter, Marina—but his emergence was mostly a reflection of the disaffection among the boyar groups, primarily, no doubt, the Romanovs, who ultimately benefited by his enterprise. The whole Romanov clan had been accused by Godunov of having used witchcraft in an attempt to usurp Godunov's crown; the head of the family, Theodore Romanov, father of the future Tsar Michael, had been forced to become a monk, under the name of Philaret, in a distant monastery where he was kept imprisoned.

Dmitri assembled an army of some 3,500 to 4,000 men—a random assortment of Polish knights, soldiers of fortune, and runaway Russian peasants. Polish complicity enabled Dmitri to organize this group on Polish terrain, but the army's quick successes were due not to Polish support but to the feebleness of the Moscow regime. The unruly Cossacks and discontented small landowners of the southern regions went over to Dmitri in a body, as did many of the petty nobles and burghers; the Russians in fact engulfed the small Polish core of his army. When Godunov died unexpectedly in 1605, the pretender made a triumphal entry into Moscow.

Boris Godunov. XVIth century miniature. This wily Tatar regent made himself Tsar in 1598. Surrounded by plots, driven by dark suspicions, he established an early version of the police state based on a network of informers. He was a favorite figure for Russian writers. Pushkin and Mussorgsky immortalized him in an opera.

But the False Dmitri's anti-Godunov coalition fell apart at once because of its contradictory composition. The boyars hoped for a restoration of their ancient privileges; the petty nobles wanted bigger land-grants, more money, and a tighter grip on the peasants working their estates; the peasants, especially the Cossacks, longed for land and freedom; the foreign mercenaries clamored for their pay; the Jesuits and Polish clericals intrigued for a reunion of the two churches under the Vatican.

These conflicting currents undid the pretender, who was murdered by May 1606, as they ruined the next Tsar, Basil Shuisky, who was appointed by the aristocracy without even a pretense of formality. A scion of the senior branch of the house of Rurik, with no reservations about absolutism, Basil represented, socially speaking, the people who had appointed him, which immediately made him the target of the radically inclined Cossack masses and small landowners.

For the first time in Russian history, a movement of disaffection was launched that injected a social element into the dynastic conflicts. A runaway slave, Ivan Bolotnikov, rallied the fugitive peasants and slaves who made up the main body of the Cossacks, and under the guise of restoring Dmitri he proclaimed a program of social revolution, which included the slaughter of the upper classes, the incitement of the poor against the rich and of the peasants and slaves against their masters, and the redistribution of the land, wealth, and women held by the oppressors.

This movement, which fought, oddly enough, together with a detachment of some of the petty service-nobility, came within sight of Moscow by October 1606; here, as it turned out, the very extremism of Bolotnikov's movement enabled Tsar

Boris Shuisky to rally around himself the proprietary and conservative groups appalled by Bolotnikov's aims. Bolotnikov quickly lost his allies among the nobility; his movement was suppressed by the most savage means. The rebel provinces, about a third of the country, were flung open to plunder; thousands of prisoners were executed, a great many by slow drowning, a peculiarly cruel form of torture.

Pretenders sprang up like mushrooms in 1607–8. A score of rebels took the name of Tsarevich: imaginations were strained to provide the flimsiest of connections with the Moscow dynasty. The most effective of these pretenders became famous as the Tushino Bandit, so called from the location of his headquarters, set up in the spring of 1608, in Tushino, a few miles from Moscow. Even less is known about this second False Dmitri, as he was also known, than about the first. In his case there was not even a pretense of belief in his dynastic claims. To be sure, the names taken by all the impostors were merely a pretext for attacking the official regime.

Shuisky appealed to foreign governments for help, as well as to the Russian cities whose support he could depend on. But perhaps the chief reason for the failure of the Tushino Bandit's rebellion was its invasion of the northern provinces, which were not so disaffected as the southern and had continued to enjoy a slight degree of self-government, which was disregarded entirely by the Polish mercenaries, Russian gentry, and Cossacks in the Bandit's entourage. Even the northern peasants resented the bandit's savagery; by 1610 the siege of Moscow had fallen apart.

For two years Tushino played the role of a second capital because of the radical instability of Shuisky's regime. An unusual number of boyars, churchmen, nobles, functionaries, merchants, and commoners kept switching back and forth between Tushino and Moscow, hoping for the best. As the price of their slippery support, they traded the grants and promotions they managed to secure from Shuisky for still greater benefits from the Bandit, and the other way around. It was the desperation of both camps and the country's exhaustion that made this situation possible. One of the chief notables in the Bandit's camp, for instance, was Philaret Romanov who, while presumably a prisoner, was revered by the insurgents as their patriarch.

When things looked black for the Bandit, Philaret Romanov and the Tushino aristocracy turned to Poland and signed an agreement in February 1610 that made the Polish King's son Tsar of Muscovy while ensuring the inviolability of the existing Russian state and the Orthodox Church.

Shuisky finally had to abdicate. Polish troops occupied Moscow and the Kremlin, whereupon Sigismund, the King of Poland, made an attempt to get the throne for himself, not his son. This infuriated everyone; in addition it aroused the anti-Catholic mood of the masses, and for that matter irritated the Swedes, who had joined the Polish-led anti-Shuisky coalition while at the same time becoming rivals of the Poles on the Baltic coast. (The Swedes actually launched a False Dmitri of their own.)

From the Russian point of view, the Protestant Swedes in Novgorod, the Catholic Poles in Moscow, and the huge bands of brigands roaming about the country were a sign of utter political devastation. This chaos was finally ended by a popular uprising, instigated, curiously enough, by a wealthy butcher, Kuzma Minin, who together with a Prince Pozharsky defeated the Poles. Russia was confronted by the urgent need of settling once and for all on a Tsar who would be genuinely accepted.

A Territorial Assembly began forming in Moscow in January 1613; though there is hardly any information about it, this may be the first representative group ever to have convened there. The numerous candidates for the throne included many foreigners, among them some Habsburgs, but eventually Michael Romanov, a quite unknown boy of sixteen, was elected in February and proclaimed Tsar.

Michael was chosen as a compromise between conservative and radical elements. He was favored partly because of his family status, since the Romanovs were related to the house of Rurik and had been immersed in Moscow court affairs for a few hundred years; he was also a nephew of Ivan the Terrible's son, Theodore: both factors made him

Tsar Michael Romanov (1613–1645). The Time of Troubles came to an end with the Poles pushed out of Moscow and the boyars electing young Michael Romanov Tsar—the first of this dynasty to occupy the throne. The new ruler was grandnephew of Ivan the Terrible. Anonymous Russian painting, XVIIth century.

attractive to the legitimists. From a different angle, since his father Philaret had been made Metropolitan of Rostov by the first False Dmitri and Patriarch by the second, the Romanovs were ensured the backing of the Cossacks.

But perhaps what promoted Michael's candidacy most was his insignificance. This was taken by many of his backers at the Territorial Assembly to mean pliability. He was so little known that the delegation sent by the Assembly to offer him the crown had no idea where he was.

In spite of all the social turmoil that had been going on for fifteen years, the new Tsar ascended the throne with no limitation whatsoever on his power. He was invested with all the traditional absolutism of the autocracy developed by Ivan the Terrible and his forebears.

For that matter, the country had not changed in the slightest during the preceding period of anarchy; it was the same, only more exhausted. It had had a social upheaval expressed in various ways and under various leaders with an unmistakable element of revolutionary unrest; dynasties had changed kaleidoscopically, foreign powers had invaded the country, there had been the devastation, impoverishment, and slaughter typical of civil wars, but nothing had been changed in the state structure. Indeed, though it was undoubtedly the revolutionary nature of the Time of Troubles, both comprehensive and profound, that accounts for the extravagant churning up of the whole country, the strangest thing about it is the total subsidence of the whole movement. The masses of peasants and slaves were given back to their masters; the institution of serfdom emerged from the chaos rejuvenated and stronger than ever—the foundation of the Muscovite state.

Nor did the number of parvenus represent a change in the state's structure. On the contrary, the Time of Troubles, which had accelerated the political decomposition of the old boyar and princely families, merely replaced them with a different group of service-nobles who owed their wealth and power to the Tsar's favor. This rounded off a process begun with the unification of the realm under Ivan the Terrible's immediate forebears and consummated by his *oprichnina*.

The formation of this new social group, distinct from the old families, had been well advanced during the sixteenth century; the Time of Troubles made the process irrevocable. For that matter the parvenus who had rocketed to the surface wanted to make themselves respectable as quickly as possible; they had no interest in overhauling society. As for the Church, throughout the storm and stress of the civil war, neither its vast estates nor its old privileges were touched.

During the sixteenth century the growth of serfdom was accentuated by some other factors. The practice, formerly permitted, of serving a lord personally without losing one's personal liberty—distinct from tenancy, since it had nothing to do with the use of land—was drastically reduced. The celebrated Code of Laws *(Ulozhenie)* of 1649 laid down that anyone who served a lord even for three months renounced his status as a freeman. It also became usual during the second quarter of the seventeenth century for a tenant to give his landlord a written promise to live on the land assigned him until his death: this amounted to a renunciation of his former right to give up his tenancy, which meant that the tenant's dependence on his landlord, formerly based on his indebtedness, now assumed the character of a contract.

This was a reflection of the government's need to pin down its taxpayers, since peasants still paid taxes and did so even after becoming serfs.

But the peasants could still run away; the government constricted them still further, in the Code of 1649, by abolishing any limit on the time runaways could be searched for. This enabled squires to recover runaway peasants whenever they found them and riveted the tenant to his landlord even more strongly than before. What had been a contractual relation now became a hereditary one backed by law.

In fact, from the middle of the seventeenth century on, what had once been a clear-cut line of division between former peasant tenants and slaves tended to vanish, despite the survival of some technicalities that were not wiped out until a decree of January 1723 laid a poll-tax on the whole servile population.

This hunt was naturally taken up by the peasants themselves: landlords were assassinated right and left, manor houses burnt. The situation reached an extreme point in the revolt, still celebrated in folk-songs today, of Stenka Razin, who started a campaign against Moscow in the summer of 1670. Once again this campaign was not aimed at the Tsar but at the boyars and landlords. Peasants rushed to slaughter their masters and joined Razin *en masse*, but despite his initial successes, which gave him control of the Volga River from its mouth to Simbirsk, and after exterminating landlords wholesale, he was defeated and executed in 1671.

Razin's movement had been typically spontaneous and shapelessly ferocious. Its persistence as a motif in the folk imagination doubtless reflects the permanence of conditions underlying Razin's career; the legend has it that he miraculously escaped death, eluded his executioners, and turned up a century later during the reign of Catherine the Great. The paradox of Razin's career was characteristic of Russian society of the time—while even the most extremist elements of society vehemently proclaimed their devotion to the crown, the Tsar himself was in terror of his own people.

With rare exceptions, the Russian upper classes had no education at all. If the boyar could read, he read nothing but works of piety or a romance translated from some foreign language; there were no native writers. The rich folk-lore and folk-literature of the peasants, an immense cultural treasure-house, was completely outside the interests or knowledge of the upper classes. Both Nikonians and Old Believers had the same attitude: while the latter rejected any changes at all, however trivial, the Nikonians themselves believed solely in a return to the Greek source of the religion. Both parties were incapable of intellectualizing their positions by devising new ideas; thus both clung to the dead letter of essentially unintelligible doctrines.

For centuries Russia was a unique combination of dreariness, coarseness, and brutality. Debauchery, drunkenness, and illiteracy were universal. The courtiers around the sovereign were not courtiers in any European sense; there was nothing sociable about the life of the court. Upper-class women, including the Tsarina, were secluded in a Byzantine type of harem: they never went out unless heavily veiled; they looked on at palace ceremonies from behind a gallery grillwork. The Kremlin had the aspect of a convent, night-club, and shop simultaneously. Church services were frequent and long, drinking on feast-days was tremendous, and Russian noblemen spent most of their time discussing sales of hemp, furs, and tar.

Even the first Romanovs had used foreigners to develop Russia's much needed natural resources. It was plain to the few thoughtful members of the upper class that something had to be done to reform Russia, if only technically. Out of the seventy years between the first Romanov's accession and the death of Peter the Great's father, the Muscovite autocracy was at war for about thirty, sometimes fighting on several fronts at once. It had focussed the attention of both the rebellious masses and liberally-minded upper-class individuals on its slovenliness. A change of pace and direction was needed, a serious effort to catch up with and pass the West, to use a phrase put forward by the Soviet government more than two hundred years later.

This change was begun by Peter the Great; by the time he appeared, Russia had fallen so far behind that the whole of society seemed to need recasting. Peter was to encounter opposition, but it must be recalled that he was backed by the bulk of the service-nobility and a small but active minority of the mercantile community. The conventional picture of Peter as a titan fighting against terrible odds on behalf of civilization, or conversely of a tyrant obliged to overcome universal recalcitrance, is highly misleading.

Peter was born in 1672, the fourteenth child of the pious Tsar Alexis by his second wife, a member of the Naryshkin clan. Alexis' first wife had been a Miloslavsky, by whom he had three sons and six daughters; the resulting situation was so confused, that when Alexis' first son died in 1682 after a brief reign, it triggered a flare-up of intrigues between the two clans.

In the Russia of his time Peter might have come from another planet, or even from nineteenth-century America. He had an altogether secular, democratic view of life. Physically huge, with fabulous energy and stamina, he grew up completely outside of and indifferent to the traditional life of Muscovy. He was self-made; he never learned any grammar or spelling, and had scarcely any formal education.

He was soon enthralled by the purely material achievements of European civilization in the form of the scraps of technical information he picked up hanging about the motley assortment of expatriates in the Foreign Suburb, which he became familiar with before he was twenty. He made his first contact with Western civilization, in fact, through a friendship with a Dutch seaman; throughout his life he retained the dress, speech, and bearing of his first Western tutor. Western Europe, as represented in the Foreign Suburb, dominated his mind as long as he lived.

As a boy Peter lived most of his life in a small village, where he collected a large group of young men of the lowest social origins to drill with. Beginning when he was only eleven years old, though exceptionally well developed, he turned them into the nucleus of a military force. His taste for low companions continued throughout his life; one of the "stableboys," a childhood friend he seems to have been in love with, the illiterate, unscrupulous, ambitious, and beautiful Menshikov, who had started life as a street-peddler, was one of the most powerful figures in the state even after Peter's death.

Peter's inner circle was bound together by liquor and debauchery. Their orgies were distinguished by a complicated and imaginative ceremonial devised by Peter. Unlike other interests, erratic and fleeting, these orgies remained a constant preoccupation.

When he was eighteen he organized his disreputable associates in a sort of satirical society called "The Most Drunken

Assembly of Fools and Jesters," sworn to the worship of Venus and Bacchus and with an elaborate ceremonial parodying both the Roman Catholic and the Greek Orthodox Churches. In this drunken hierarchy, Peter was a mere deacon. This ostentatious humbling of himself was characteristic. In the procession celebrating his first signal military success, the capture of Azov on the Black Sea, he marched in the ranks himself, dressed as a naval captain.

There are voluminous records in Peter's own hand describing the structure and activities of this Assembly. People had to take part in public celebrations in which a stellar role was assigned the Assembly, or else they would be liable to severe punishment. Parades and masquerades that lasted for days on end had to be attended by the royal family and court and state functionaries, as well as by diplomats, all playing peculiar musical instruments and all in costume. Peter would be present dressed as a Dutch seaman and pounding away at his favorite instrument, the drums. Toward the end of his reign these enforced celebrations became more and more common.

He had a weakness for arranging pseudo-weddings for which he would contrive fantastic and obscene rituals. When one of the two heads of the Assembly, Zotov, a septuagenarian drunkard, formerly Peter's tutor, who had been given the mock title of Pope or Patriarch of the Assembly, was "married," the preparations for the mock ceremony kept everyone at court and in the government busy for months; Peter himself supervised every detail. In the thick of his war with Sweden, Peter never neglected his ribald, silly correspondence with his drunken friends.

Coat of arms of Russia and the Russian provinces at the time of Peter the Great. Korb "Diarium Itineris in Moscoviam."

Historians have naturally devoted a good deal of effort to extracting some point from this curious rigmarole. It is a futile enterprise; the Assembly was exactly what it sounds like.

Peter was very free-and-easy in his manner, with a peculiar sense of humor. On noticing his friends' disgust during a visit to an anatomical laboratory in Holland, he made them tear a corpse to shreds with their bare teeth. Once, on overhearing a maid-in-waiting to the Tsarina complain of a wasted youth, he gave her a lesson first hand, in front of the whole court, in the sexual experience she had missed.

At the age of twenty-four Peter decided to see Western Europe for himself. After imposing himself on the attention of European governments by defeating the Turks in an impromptu campaign, he set out on his own idea of a grand tour. He had already shown his interest in foreign countries by resuming the practice of Boris Godunov of sending young Russians abroad for study, but he was the first Russian sovereign to leave his country on a peaceful mission since the legendary Princess Olga's trip to Constantinople in the tenth century.

At the European courts he visited, he struck everyone as most peculiar: his behavior was bizarre, his anger volcanic, his person sloppy, his manners nonexistent, and his attitude toward knives and forks hostile.

Peter had upset enough people in Russia for a dissident movement to spring up. Shortly before he left for Western Europe, in March 1697, a conspiracy against him was discovered. It involved the "Archers" *(Streltsy)* and the Cossacks, and was aimed at reinstating Peter's older half-sister Sophie, who had been enabled to rule as regent while Peter had still been a boy.

Portrait of Catherine, second wife of Peter the Great, as a young woman. She was a Baltic servant girl who had been his friend Menshikov's mistress. After bearing the Tsar four illegitimate children they were married, to the scandal of the court. Catherine made a most devoted wife.

After Peter's unexpected return to Moscow he started a reign of terror unheard of since Ivan the Terrible. He personally kept fourteen torture chambers busy twenty-four hours a day; in an attempt to involve Sophie and his other half-sisters in the plot he personally, together with his intimates and henchmen, tortured more than seventeen hundred people. But in spite of great imaginativeness, he failed to get enough evidence. The tortures were followed by mass executions, hundreds of people being killed. Peter led his friends in the head-lopping. The corpses were left to rot in public for five months. One hundred and ninety-seven were hanged in the convent where Sophie was imprisoned, three in front of her window, their dead hands clinging to letters allegedly written to her by the Archers.

Peter then left Moscow for a few days; when he came back in January 1699 the slaughter was resumed with equal savagery, preceded by a riotous celebration of the Most Drunken Assembly, including a particularly obscene masquerade, to open a new and luxurious mansion Peter had had built for one of his oldest friends, Lefort, a Swiss. After paying their respects to Venus and Bacchus, the merrymakers surged back to the torture chambers, execution blocks, and gallows. By the end of February, more than a thousand mutilated bodies had been taken away. The Archers were shattered.

This extravaganza of ferocity was accompanied, typically enough, by Peter's first spectacular attempt to Westernize Russia, or at least the shaving customs of the upper classes. The day after his return, Peter showed himself in Western dress in public and took a pair of shears to the flowing beards of the court dignitaries. This was bound to inflame sentiment. A beard was of the utmost importance to pious Muscovites; the Russian Church taught that it was indispensable to the "image of God" in which man was made. Its loss therefore meant that people were no better than cats and dogs. That led to eternal damnation.

This was only one of the many shocks reserved for Peter's generation. His effort to transform Russia sprang out of his preoccupation with warfare. When he found himself confronted by better organized armies in the West, he was led, shortsightedly and planlessly, into an assault on the whole social structure. Out of the thirty-five years of his reign, only the last year, 1724, was free of war; the rest of the time Russia was at peace for only thirteen months. These wars were not imposed on him in any way; he launched them arbitrarily, with no clear view of their aims.

His most demonstrative attempt at catching up with the West had to do with changing the way Russians looked. His cutting the beards of the court functionaries in 1698, after coming back from Western Europe, turned out to be not merely one of the pranks the young Tsar was famous for, but the beginning of a systematic regime of savagely enforced modernization in the dress and appearance of the boyars, the nobility, and for that matter the entire city population. Decrees in 1700 and 1701 ordered all these classes to adopt "Hungarian" dress, and all men and women, except the clergy and peasants, to wear "German, Saxon, or French" clothes on pain of "cruel punishments." By 1705 most of the upper classes had yielded, though for a time the aristocracy preferred its traditional high bonnets and long robes with flowing sleeves.

Peter launched an immense series of cultural reforms, beginning with the reform of the calendar, which reckoned time since the beginning of the world and started the year with September. This calendar, an object of veneration, especially to the Old Believers, was changed in 1699 to the Julian calendar. The first Russian newspaper appeared in 1703, and in 1708 the alphabet was simplified. But the retention of the ancient Slavonic alphabet for the Church accentuated the alienation between the Church and other educated groups that was to leave its stamp on intellectual evolution.

Peter thought geometry the key to all knowledge; since his interests in general had a narrowly practical tinge, there was a steady output of dictionaries and translations of textbooks on arithmetic, geometry, fortification, etc. No literature was published to speak of. The light side of life was coped with in a book on etiquette translated from German; since the Russians had been commanded to behave according to Peter's view of polite society, the book was very popular.

Peter made a tremendous effort to launch higher education, at least his own version of it, which was formed largely by his obsession with navigation and related studies, but he kept colliding with a currently irremediable absence of textbooks and properly trained teachers and the equally marked absence of pupils. School discipline was grotesquely harsh even for the period; most parents were reluctant to allow their children to get an education. The student quota, laid down by fiat, was difficult to fill; the schools were ignored by the potential students *en masse.*

The entire conception of an educational program was lopsided. At a time when the country had no schools worth mentioning, either elementary or secondary, Peter, apparently inspired by Leibniz, arranged to launch a Russian Academy of Science. Seventeen professors were imported from Germany, but since no Russians were qualified to take the courses, some eight students had to be scraped up in Germany too, and as this number was not enough to listen to the seventeen professors' lectures, the professors were obliged to attend each other's. The oddity is that in spite of everything the scholarly ability of the first fellows was quite respectable; after Peter's death the capital benefited by this novel note of intellectual life.

Peter did not abolish the privileges of the aristocracy; he simply formalized the old Russian concept of state service. The originally clear distinction between patrimonial estates, owned outright by the nobles, and estates subject to service had been confounded for some time; Peter wiped it out altogether. A decree of 1721 made every army officer an hereditary noble regardless of origin; the concept was developed and ramified in a decree of the following year that established the celebrated Table of Ranks. This included an attribution of personal lifetime nobility, a notion curiously at variance with any Western European concept. The upshot was that you were no longer an officer because you were noble, but noble because you were an officer. All landowners became nobles with the same obligations to the state; the distinction between the great and the petty nobility vanished.

The Table of Ranks drew a clear line, for the first time, between civilian and military service. All officers in each of these two branches were put into a hierarchical order of fourteen classes, each of which had to be passed through, beginning from the bottom. The Table of Ranks extended the privilege of hereditary ennoblement to civil servants who had attained a certain rank.

The Table of Ranks was one of Peter's must durable reforms. It gave a sharp outline to the bureaucratic state that had begun developing in Muscovy even before him, and it created a bureaucratic tradition that was to survive the upheaval of 1917. Peter replaced the easy-going sloppiness of patriarchal Muscovy by a ramified system of protocol and etiquette, ranks, titles, emblems of obsequiousness, and above all of uniforms. These became compulsory for anyone even remotely connected with the state; they were worn by civil servants as well as by army officers, and later on by students, including secondary-school students of both sexes. On its upper levels the country became a sort of gigantic barrack-house. Though the pervasive regimentation was relaxed to some extent during the liberalization of the upper classes in the nineteenth century, it never entirely disappeared.

Despite his fabulous energy Peter's mind was elementary. Utterly "practical," he had no grasp of general ideas. Though he has gone down in history as the great Reformer (or rather Transformer), he never had any real plan. He was merely obsessed by a desire to catch up with the West technologically; it was because of his determination to combine this general obsession with his other obsession for warmaking that he had to initiate an immense variety of changes in government and taxation to carry on his wars. Though he was quick and inquisitive, his ignorance was fatal. Since his obsession was always with a practical goal, and since he was incapable of formulating general principles, his method was inevitably one of trial and error, nearly always error. His practical policies generally cancelled each other out.

Peter was a combination of vast energy, practicality, and intellectual limitation; his reforms were both artificial and fragmentary. By failing to perceive that civilization underlies technology, not vice-versa, and that traditional Russian institutions eluded the superficial control of his administrative improvisations, he ran head-on into an almost solid wall of resistance.

His reforms were fragmentary in any case; they touched only a minute class. Not only did the Russian masses remain inert and lethargic as before, since in their vast numbers Peter could conceive of them only as targets of the knout, but Peter alienated the upper classes from the masses far more completely than occurred elsewhere by forcing Russia into the forms of Western culture. The comfortable national identity of ignorance, squalor, and coarseness, based on an identity of customs and beliefs, yielded to a society divided by a broader chasm than before. In order to live up to Peter's demands the landed nobility had to extract even more from their serfs; the functionaries of the more streamlined bureaucracy were tamer than ever. Together they constituted the summit of society. Underneath them lay the people, groaning.

A vivid expression of popular bile may be more appropriate than a lofty summing-up of Peter the Great's career. An instance of cheap lithography, one of the few artistic media accessible to the masses, has survived in a poster showing a cat being buried by mice. It is a bitter satire on Peter, his court and his reforms, and on the extravagant display of official grief at his death. The poster surely reflects an opinion widespread in practically every social group. It is in sharp contrast to the dithyrambs of professional historians.

The cat buried by mice, XVIIIth century Russian caricature of Peter the Great, represented here as a fat cat. Political satire appeared for the first time in the XVIIIth century. This famous popular print, instigated by the Old Believers who saw Peter as the Antichrist himself, was a thinly disguised jibe at his funeral (1725), with the eight horses pulling the hearse transformed into eight mice.

CHAPTER V

CATHERINE THE GREAT

During the thirty-seven years between the reigns of Peter the Great and Catherine the Great, the Russian throne was occupied by a grotesque assembly of ignorant sluts, feebleminded German princes, and children, a total of seven rulers in all, each representing the power of the Guards regiments founded by Peter, which remained a decisive factor for some time.

With no stable principle of authority, and with a variety of contending elements of power, policy in St. Petersburg increasingly became a football of competing cliques, especially since the country had acquired international consequence. The political horizon was no longer confined to parochial disputes with Turkey, Poland, and Sweden; St. Petersburg was now a factor in Western Europe as well.

It must have been obvious that the Guards would have the last word in deciding who was to ascend the throne; during Peter's last illness they were sounded out to see whether they would help keep his widow Catherine on the throne. Catherine, who had accompanied Peter on so many campaigns, was popular with the army, both officers and men; troops thought to favor her were rushed to the capital. Their approval of Catherine was stimulated by the simple device of giving them their pay, by now almost a year and a half in arrears, and promising them future rewards with understandable generosity.

This simple procedure established a mold for the palace revolutions that characterized the eighteenth century. During the forty years after Peter the Great's death, the throne was claimed by his grandson Peter; his two daughters by Catherine, Anne and Elizabeth, born out of wedlock; and his three nieces, Catherine, Anne, and Praskovie (the last of whom played no political role). The success of one or another depended on the decision, enforced by the Guards regiments, of a clique of fortuitously organized higher officials.

Coronation of Empress Anne (1730), from an album printed in Moscow the same year. After Peter the Great's death (1725) the crown passed in rapid succession to his widow, his grandson, then to his niece Anne, widowed Duchess of Courland.

Since Catherine did not pretend to rule but simply devoted herself to debauchery of one kind or another, Menshikov, one of Peter's favorites who had been instrumental in putting her on the throne, remained the chief power in the land. He managed to consolidate his power still further after Catherine's death in May 1727 by marrying his daughter to Peter's young grandson. A document signed by Catherine (now regarded as a forgery) provided for still another bizarre departure from the monarchical principle—the throne was to pass to the grandson, Peter II, and his line, or in case of its extinction to Catherine's two daughters, Anne of Holstein and her line or Elizabeth and her line. The daughters of the senior line, by Peter the Great's feebleminded brother and short-lived co-Tsar, Ivan V, were passed over in silence. On Catherine's death, Menshikov's prospective son-in-law, Peter II, was hailed at the age of eleven as Emperor.

But Menshikov's career, seemingly at its peak, failed to live up to its prospects. The arrogance of the "overbearing Goliath," as he was called, had multiplied his enemies beyond control. He had alienated the young Emperor and even lost his hold over the Guards in whose ranks he had started out. Only three months later, after a short illness, he was banished with his whole family, ultimately to Siberia.

The dynastic situation remained as amorphous as ever. After considering the various candidates mentioned above, the Supreme Privy Council, plus a number of other highly placed people, arbitrarily selected Anne, Duchess of Courland, second daughter of Ivan V, Peter's brother and former co-Tsar, apparently because she was considered a model of submissiveness.

Anne was thirty-seven at the time. Married at the age of seventeen to the Duke of Courland, she was widowed only a few weeks after the marriage; she had been obliged to spend nineteen years in the eccentric position of a duchess without a duchy. A bigoted, highly sensual ignoramus, she was dependent on the niggardly subsidies of the Russian court, whose agent was in charge of the duchy. All this time she had been writing humble, illiterate notes to her imperial relatives and to the favorites in power. When she finally found herself on the throne after this lengthy and generally hopeless-looking exile, she quickly made up for lost time.

She had been involved in a liaison with Ernst Johann Biron (Bühren), a minor functionary of German descent, who was supposed to be dropped on her return to Russia; like the other conditions, however, this was also disregarded. Biron became the real ruler of Russia during her reign (actually known in Russian history as the *Bironovshchina*—the Biron era).

The moment she became Empress, Anne flung aside the docile impersonation she had been forced to carry on for so long and plunged into an unflagging series of splendid palace and church festivities. She had inherited Peter the Great's predilection for peculiar people: she filled the imperial residences not only with animals, especially those that could perform amusing tricks, but with all sorts of giants, midgets, cripples, beggars, and clowns. She kept a large corps of women on hand who did nothing but entertain her by telling stories. Anne also had Peter the Great's liking for practical jokes and satirical rites: she celebrated a "marriage" between two princes, a Golitsyn and a Volkonsky; years later she made this Golitsyn the bridegroom of a famously repulsive Kalmyk woman in a grotesque ceremony performed in a palace made of ice.

In accordance with Anne's often proclaimed motto of ruling in the "spirit of Peter the Great," she moved the court and government back to St. Petersburg the year after her accession, putting an end to the short-lived experiment of reviving Moscow as capital.

As part of a campaign to crush the Dolgorukis, Golitsyns, and other great clans who had attempted to curb the autocracy in their own interests, Anne intensified the police terror. Once again the torture chambers began ingesting their quota of people, often on the mere suspicion of disapproval of Anne's regime; thousands were sent to Siberia, often to vanish completely.

Anne remained childless; as she began to fall ill toward the end of her reign, the regime was again confronted by a dynastic muddle. This was given a stop-gap solution by the birth of an heir to Anne's niece, Princess Anna Leopoldovna of Mecklenburg, the only descendant of the senior Romanov branch. Biron had attempted to anchor himself more firmly in the ruling circle by marrying his son to young Anna Leopoldovna, but he was unable to withstand the opposition of his rivals and the unwillingness of the bride herself, who chose to marry a German prince (Anthony of Brunswick-Bevern-Luneburg) for whom also she had no liking. This match produced a boy in August 1740; before Anne died a few months later, she appointed the infant her heir. The best Biron managed out of this was his appointment as regent until the baby, called Ivan VI, reached the age of seventeen.

Throughout Princess Anna's regency, the contention for the helm of Russia between various German cliques and individuals was incessant; it was brought to an end only by a palace revolution at the end of 1741 that resulted in the arrest of the

Brunswick family, the deposition of the infant Ivan VI, and the accession to the throne of Peter the Great's daughter Elizabeth, thirty years old.

Elizabeth was to reign for twenty years, until her death in 1762. Peter the Great, hoping to fit her for a major role at the court of Versailles, had taught her German, French, and dancing; otherwise she was uneducated.

Contemporaries considered her beauty and charm irresistible. Gay and amorous, she concentrated exclusively and with a disconcerting lack of inhibition on carnal amusements. Lightminded and irresponsible, she seems to have frequented the Guards' barracks for simple pleasure rather than in pursuit of any elaborate political objectives, but her charming accessibility nevertheless created a faithful following for her among the Guardsmen, who were used to regarding the throne as their private preserve. Those who were against the Brunswick family and the German connection generally took advantage of her entourage. St. Petersburg, now deeply involved in European affairs, was an arena for power politics; it suited France and Sweden to use Elizabeth and her Guardsmen as a means of getting rid of politicians whom they could easily claim to be alien to Russia's interests without harping unnecessarily on their own.

Elizabeth's rule brought life in St. Petersburg much nearer to the European model the elite were longing for so ardently. The festivities were far more conventional. The relays of masquerades, spectacles, and hunts were no longer marred by the grotesqueries of Empress Anne's reign. The cripples and clowns had vanished, while Elizabeth's beloved Guardsmen did much to elevate the standard of looks if not urbanity around the court.

Medal commemorating the oaths exchanged between the Preobrazhensky Guards and Elizabeth, youngest daughter of Peter the Great, in 1741. Elizabeth was brought to the throne after conspiracies between the French ambassador and dissatisfied elements at court led to a palace revolution that banished the infant Tsar and his mother and got rid of the hated German officials. Medals Department, Bibliothèque Nationale, Paris.

But with all the changes of regime during the period of turmoil that followed the death of Peter the Great, with all the personal corruption of the series of backstage favorites, with all the capriciousness of the policies that emerged through the complex filtering-chamber of the alliances with German houses, there was, nevertheless, a certain unity of development. Serfdom progressed steadily; not only did it become more comprehensive, but it also became a hallmark of class privilege. The monarchs who succeeded Peter the Great, especially his daughter Elizabeth, confronted one peasant rebellion after another. These uprisings were especially frequent and savage on the monasteries' estates and in the industrial enterprises worked by serfs. It was a common occurrence for great bands of armed peasants, numbering sometimes several thousand, to wage pitched battles with the punitive expeditions sent against them. The private soldiers, who were subject to a life term of service, often joined them, only to be overcome ultimately by still other government troops. Every uprising was crushed; its leaders were all killed on the wheel, the gallows, or the whipping post, or deported to the Siberian wilderness.

A palace revolution put Catherine the Great on the throne for thirty-four years. Born Princess of Anhalt-Zerbst, she ascended the throne over her murdered husband Peter III, with the support of the Preobrazhensky Regiment. Peter III has a peculiarly bad reputation (chiefly because of Catherine's tireless literary energies), having come down in history as a depraved and drunken moron, but his chief political shortcoming seems to have been that he was one of the few Russian monarchs in the eighteenth century to mount the throne legally; hence he had no effective support at all. Catherine herself was wholly a usurper: she could at most have claimed to hold the throne as regent for her son Paul. But after Peter III was murdered, apparently with Catherine's at least tacit approval, Catherine, though nothing whatever was known about her outside the court, clung successfully to the throne.

Catherine II has come down as one of the most glamorous monarchs in history. This is largely due to her talent and zeal for press agentry. Also her position enabled her to hire the services of still more talented press agents such as Voltaire. One of her cardinal objectives was to be on friendly terms with Voltaire, Diderot, and d'Alembert, not only through snobbery but because she saw clearly how useful such indefatigable writers and opinion-molders could be in singing her praises. As Frederick II said, she was "very proud, very ambitious, and very vain."

Voltaire, unusually available, became a completely pliant instrument of her wishes. He praised her at all times and endorsed everything she did, lauding the first partition of

Poland as a victory of "tolerance" over "fanaticism." Much the same was done by his colleagues and the growing band of their Russian followers. By acquiring the public support of internationally known French writers and thinkers, Catherine thus secured her position at home.

Nine days after Catherine took power she invited Diderot to shift to Russia the publication of the *Encyclopédie,* suspended in France. A few years later she bought Diderot's library, allowing him to keep the books and draw a pension of 1,000 livres as Her Majesty's Librarian. This openhanded policy paid off richly; such acts are the underpinnings of Catherine's reputation for enlightenment. After Diderot's visit to Russia in 1773, he gave Catherine *carte blanche* in the way of moral support and praised her as combining "the soul of Brutus with the charm of Cleopatra."

Favoritism had always had a lush growth at the Russian court; Catherine made it a semi-official institution. Her ten chief favorites, in succession, were given apartments next to hers and treated magnificently: titles, lucrative estates, and vast fortunes were the index of her affections. An oddity of hers was an absence of vindictiveness toward her lovers for straying; nor did she persecute the lovers she sacked. Among her lovers, Orlov, Potyomkin, and Zubov were powerful influences on government policy, both domestic and foreign.

Potyomkin's power outlived his love affair; he influenced Catherine until his death. He was mysteriously skillful in influencing the choice of his successors, who were nearly all his tools. For years he was an all-powerful counselor of Catherine's; he was one of the inspirers of her ambitious project for the expulsion of the Turks from Europe.

Prince Gregory Orlov was Catherine's lover while she was still Grand Duchess, one of five brothers who conspired to do away with Peter and enthrone Catherine. Painted by the Italian artist S. Torelli.

In spite of her frivolous early education, Catherine became a voracious reader during the seclusion forced on her under the reign of her aunt-in-law, the Empress Elizabeth. She was also an indefatigable, thoroughly mediocre writer of tragedies, comedies, polemical works, musical comedy librettos, treatises on pedagogy, allegorical tales, and historical writings, as well as her memoirs, which have become celebrated. Her collected works, apart from her vast correspondence and her celebrated *Instruction*—a philosophical draft constitution for Russia—fill a dozen bulky volumes. Though her Russian was good enough for speaking, it was scarcely a literary medium—her ideas about grammar and spelling were vague. (In a very common Russian word of only three letters, she made four mistakes in spelling.) As for what she wrote in French, it was all thoroughly processed and corrected in the most modern manner before being released.

During her reign, Russia added some 200,000 square miles to its area; it was firmly established on the shores of the Baltic and the Black seas. Russia's population increased substantially, partly through these territorial acquisitions, from 19 million in 1762 to 36 million in 1796, the year of Catherine's death. This expansion cost a good deal both in lives and wealth and led to the assimilation of some peoples, such as the Tatars and Poles, who remained constant sources of disaffection. The Poles especially were a permanent target of bloody repressions.

As a matter of fact, not only did Russia's wars during the second half of the eighteenth century delay her economic development, but by extending her rule to the Polish provinces, which were never reconciled to it and in fact combated it stubbornly, these wars set up a source of disaffection very close to home. It is true that Catherine extended the boundaries of the Empire more than any other sovereign since Ivan the Terrible, but this merely heightened the contrast between the size of the realm and its underdevelopment, Russia's leitmotif for centuries.

There is a celebrated anecdote about Potyomkin's building some cheery bungalows, surrounded by merry peasants dressed in their Sunday best, in order to regale Catherine and her suite, plus some foreign diplomats, who were sailing down the Dnieper to witness the conquest of the Turks. The territory was still uninhabited, and since Potyomkin wanted to show the visitors a going concern, both the scenery and the extras were transported downstream at night and the spectacle duplicated. The story seems to be apocryphal, but its meaning is splendidly apt—all Russia was a vast Potyomkin village. It was like a brilliantly illuminated comic opera stage, with elegantly costumed lords and ladies strolling back and forth exchanging duets and witticisms in French while the mangling-machines were busily grinding away backstage.

Because Catherine was such a voluminous correspondent and gave such free expression to the loftiest ideas she could lay her hands on, the contrast between what she said and what she did is all the more striking. Despite the vast territorial expansion she is best known for, the acquisition of the littoral of the Black Sea and of new outlets on the Baltic, she failed in her attempt to undo the Ottoman Empire, not to mention her really extravagant schemes. She is reported to have said, "If I could live for 200 years, the whole of Europe would be brought under Russian rule." Also: "I shall not die before I have ejected the Turks from Europe, broken the insolence of China, and established trade relations with India."

It is true that in areas of activity where there was no danger, Catherine did try to apply some of her liberal principles as well as talk about them. She let up to some extent on the persecution of dissenters, though the question of eliminating their legal disabilities was never raised. As for the Jews, who had always been subject to a great variety of legal disabilities in addition to outright oppression on the part of the populace as well as the government, they now found their position legalized, with some negligible exceptions: they were allowed to settle in what became known as the Jewish Pale, though even there they were more heavily taxed than others. With modifications, this remained characteristic of Russia until 1917.

In fact, the second half of the eighteenth century put the landed nobility in a better position than ever. Catherine's consort had freed them from the obligation of service in 1762, and Catherine sustained this concession. Until 1785, when a new Charter of the Nobility was published, the nobles did not have to enroll in government service. They resumed life on their country estates, this time not as idlers, however, but as a group with privileges that included the direction of rural affairs. The Charter was very wordy and somewhat incoherent; it extended the privileges of the nobility and set up a framework for its corporate existence. The Charter protected the noble against deprivation of his "honor," life, property, and title (except for personal and non-hereditary titles) without a trial by his peers. Nobles could leave government service whenever they wanted to, travel abroad as much as they liked, and serve friendly foreign states. They were exempt from corporal punishment and the poll-tax, and could own houses in cities and estates with people, trade in the produce of their estates, and own industries.

Thus the emancipation of the nobility from it's previous dependence on the state made the primacy of the bureaucratic machine more unambiguous; indeed, it reinforced the vast and ramified bureaucracy that survived even the upheaval of 1917 and left its stamp on the Soviet Union.

Catherine was not merely the tool of the nobility's short-sightedness. Many landowners were aware of the dangers inherent in the plight of the peasants. On various occasions even very conservative noblemen recommended alleviations of serfdom without suggesting abolition, while the records of the abortive Legislative Commission of 1767–68 show some support for a more liberal policy on the peasant question even among the rank-and-file of the nobility. Catherine was obdurate; in her defense of what she conceived to be the interests of the class to which she owed her throne, she invariably took the most narrowminded and reactionary conception of those interests, consistently disregarding all counsels of common sense as well as of humanity. By the end of her reign, serfdom was more solidly rooted in Russian life and more grinding than ever before. Voltaire's and Montesquieu's theories were confined to the elegant conversation of a tiny circle around Empress Catherine in the opulent mansions and graceful gardens of her entourage; they were quite irrelevant to the social legislation of "the age of enlightenment."

Serfdom, though not formulated in specific legislation, was established by the end of the eighteenth century; Catherine's legislation, piecemeal though it was, consolidated it completely. Noble landowners had gradually acquired the power, not unambiguously given them by law, to dispose of their serfs as they chose. They could transport them at will, sell them with land or without, mortgage them, or settle debts with them. The sale of serfs often led to the break-up of families, condemned in principle as far back as 1721 by Peter the Great. The only legal regulation of this practice came half a century later, when Catherine stipulated that the transaction must not take place at a public auction, presumably so as not to shock her French friends. The treatment of serfs as chattels was to continue until the emancipation of 1861.

A rich landowner might have a vast number of what were called household serfs, consisting of stableboys, cooks, tailors, artists, actors, musicians, and even astronomers. The master had complete judicial authority over them except for murder and theft. The rights of possessing land and of litigation had already been taken away from the serfs by two of Catherine's predecessors; now Catherine denied them even the right to lay a complaint against their owner.

Announcements such as the following were common in contemporary newspapers: "For sale: Two domestic servants, one leatherstitcher who can also repair shoes. Thirty years of age, married: his wife is a laundress and can tend cattle; twenty-five years old. The other is a musician and singer, seventeen years of age, plays the bassoon, with a bass voice. Also for sale at same place: a Hungarian horse, three years old, very tall, English-bred, not yet ridden."

Serfs were the index of wealth: a nobleman's status was calculated in terms of the number of "registered" serfs in his possession, i.e., the number of male serfs allocated him by the preceding census.

Serfdom was not only for life but was hereditary; it could only be brought to an end by army enrollment, Siberian deportation, or emancipation voluntarily granted by the owner. The first two remedies were dependent on the owner, the superintendent of the estate, or the village council, and were probably worse than serfdom itself; the third was very rare.

A popular Russian amusement at public parks and fairs were the Sliding Hills: fun-lovers climbed up wooden steps and whizzed down a steep incline covered with ice (in summer they went down in little carts). These artificial slopes had particular appeal to northern Russians who lived in a mountainless country. Foreign artists were always intrigued by the local pastime. This scene on the frozen Neva river is by the French engraver Damane-Demartrais (1763–1827).

One of the anomalies of the period was in the serfs' economic position. Movable property, though not immune to expropriation by their masters, could be enjoyed by them as long as they owed nothing to them or to the state, and though they were forbidden to own real estate outright, there were many serfs who had *de facto* possession of town houses, populated estates, and even industrial enterprises registered in their owners' names. Serfs belonging to a great landowner, Count Sheremetiev, founded and owned many cotton mills technically belonging to him. Some serfs even accumulated large fortunes and could do as they pleased with them if they got their owners' formal agreement.

But these were of course exceptional instances. By and large there was no escape from the network of rules and customs that imprisoned most of the serfs, and when serfdom was formally introduced in the Ukraine and southeastern Russia, there was no longer any refuge from bondage.

It is this plain and simple fact that made Catherine's copy of Montesquieu's ideas in her *Instruction* a mere quip—she was repaying the landed nobility for their support by giving them free rein with their human cattle. The minor measures she passed mitigating grosser abuses, such as forbidding the enslavement of peasants once emancipated, or liberating some peasants upon the promotion of a village to a city, were more or less cancelled out by the wholesale distribution of vast troops of peasants to her favorites and generals. In fact the Russian peasantry was at the very nadir of its long and miserable existence during the reign of the Philosophers' Friend.

In reaction to this situation, the classical flight of the peasants continued without let-up; attempts to curb it, both by threats and cajolement, met with little success. Poland was one of the favorite refuges of runaway serfs until it was wiped out as a sovereign state. Catherine's foreign policy, which led to the partition of Poland and extended serfdom to the Ukraine and southeastern Russia, was welcomed with pleasure by the serf-owners. Though her regime could not remedy the conditions that provoked mass flight, it could at least block the escape hatches.

Catherine's reign marked the beginning of the French tutelage of Russian society as a whole that lasted until 1917. The

French language and a smattering of French literature became an emblem of social status and the precondition of a successful career. French tutors and private schools run by foreigners became astonishingly fashionable, so much so that any number of French barbers, coachmen from Marseilles, and often downright criminals would guide budding Russian nobles in the arts of civilization. All this took place, of course, in the summits of society. Catherine was far too taken up with expensive foreign wars and the repression of peasant uprisings to cope with the project of popular education. There were practically no schools at all. The upper classes had not yet swallowed their aversion to schools sponsored by the government; the few schools in existence could scarcely find the quota of pupils laid down for them. (Throughout Catherine's reign only one M.D. was conferred by the University of Moscow.)

The influx of influences of all kinds into Russia was matched by the exodus of noblemen abroad: their right to travel, granted by Peter III and confirmed by Catherine, for the first time gave them a chance to see Western Europe for themselves. There was a stampede to Paris, which, while offering the conventional nobleman an opportunity to ruin himself in gambling-dens, brothels, cafés, restaurants, and dress-shops, also opened the eyes of many others to Western European life, which began to change the artistic life of Russia at an increasing pace and initiated a ferment that for the next few generations was to churn up the Russian educated classes.

In the continuing blight that afflicted Russian literature throughout the seventeenth century, leaving scarcely any names worth reminding the unpedantic of, there were nevertheless two figures whose influence was disproportionate. They may be thought of as the precursors of the intelligentsia that was to play a cardinal role during the nineteenth and twentieth centuries.

The infiltration of new ideas marked the life of the Russian upper classes during the second half of the eighteenth century. These ideas, though confined to the tiny social elite, generated an intense fermentation. But just because the upper classes had adopted French language, thought, and various exotic theories, the gulf between them and their ignorant serfs was made even wider. The divergence grew progressively with the succeeding generations, as education, while encompassing more and more people in the upper strata, failed to penetrate any further. It was to have a decisive effect on the intelligentsia that developed during the nineteenth century.

The green dining room at Tsarskoye Selo, by Charles Cameron, an early example of his work for Catherine the Great. Cameron used moulded neoclassic plaster reliefs of figures, pilasters and garlands.

CHAPTER VI

TSARISM MODERNIZED

For a generation following Catherine's death, nothing changed much in Russian society, though during the reign of her grandson, Alexander I, Russia broadened the scope of her influence from mere territorial expansion in Eastern Europe and Asia and began to exercise an important, in many ways decisive, influence on all continental questions, both during and after the agitation of the Napoleonic wars. Nevertheless, things had been changing behind the smooth and lustrous facade of the Empire. An awareness of the shortcomings of absolutism began to affect even the sovereigns.

In a preamble to a plan for constitutional reform the beginning of the nineteenth century, Speransky, one Russia's few imaginative statesmen, wrote that there were only two classes in Russia: "the slaves of the autocrat and the slaves of the landowners. The former are free merely by comparison with the latter; in actual fact there are no free men in Russia except beggars and philosophers. The relationship between these two classes of slaves destroys the energy of the Russian people."

This thought had been expressed before, but it was now put into words by one of the Tsar's ministers. Though Speransky was ultimately undone by the clarity of his insight into the tangle of Russia's problems, the cleavage between illusion and fact was at last becoming unmistakable even to the topmost officials of the country.

The father of Alexander I, Paul I (1796–1801), had been cooling his heels with growing bitterness in the antechambers of the power wielded by his mother Catherine. He ascended the throne at the age of forty-three to rule a mere five years. His German-trained rigidity, and above all the drillmaster's discipline he wished to apply to the nobility as well as to the people at large, left him dangling in a vacuum, exposed to the rancor incurred by his martinet's view of the nobility's privileges.

Paul's political regime became more and more arbitrary. His hatred of republican France, one of the few tastes he shared with his deceased mother, made him heighten the oppressiveness of his regime in the wake of his declaration of war on France. Foreign books, newspapers, and even music were forbidden; foreign travel was prohibited; the censorship became even more severe and was extended even to private correspondence; functionaries were sometimes deported and degraded. In 1801, when he was murdered in his bedchamber through a plot launched by three of his intimates, undoubtedly with Alexander's consent, there was no opposition and a great deal of rejoicing.

When Alexander came to the throne, all still seemed well. Despite the somewhat bizarre circumstances of his accession—his connivance at his father's murder—there was no question of his legitimacy. Full of the French philosophy that had made his grandmother Catherine's conversation such an ornament of her salons, he had imbibed the most grandiose ideas from La Harpe, his Swiss tutor.

Born in 1777, Alexander I was brought up away from his parents under Catherine's direct supervision. A characteristic trait, his ambiguously sphinx-like charm of manner, was due doubtless to his early training. His formal schooling was ended when he was only seventeen; his teacher, La Harpe, was a fervent revolutionary in the fashion of his time, full of French radical ideas yet willing to trim his sail to the wind of autocracy.

Alexander, having learned at an early age to navigate between two conflicting winds, exemplified throughout his life the two attitudes taught him as a youth: liberalism in rhetoric and in practice devotion to the barrack-room regimentation identified with his father. His charm of manner was successful with almost everyone and in combination with his personal appearance—he was tall, fair, handsome, and limped a little from a horseback fall while young—lent him a peculiar aura of attractiveness.

Alexander's character, indeed, embodied the same contrast as his grandmother Catherine's—extravagant lip-service to the ideals of the French education they had been nurtured on, and in practical affairs an iron hand. This contrast may underlie his reputation as the "Sphinx," the "enigmatic Tsar." The French Ambassador at St. Petersburg, Count de La Ferronays, summed it up in 1820: "He talks of the rights of man, of those of peoples, and of the duties of a monarch as the disciple of a philosopher can and should talk, but at the same time he enforces his most arbitrary wishes with a greater despotism and ruthlessness than Peter the Great."

The most powerful personality associated with Alexander I was Arakcheyev (1769–1834), whose name is a synonym in Russian for ruthlessness. Arakcheyev's ascendancy coincided with that of the liberal Speransky, a coincidence that must be taken as a tribute to Alexander's simultaneously adroit and strong-willed maneuvering, since both Speransky and Arakcheyev were disliked by court and bureaucratic circles. For that matter, despite great personal differences, the universally charming Alexander and the universally loathed Arakcheyev had a great deal in common: they were both obsessed by the sort of orderliness and external symmetry achieved by close-order regimental drilling.

The condition of the peasants remained unchanged throughout Alexander's reign, the uprisings endemic in Russian life kept breaking out. When Napoleon invaded Russia in 1812, rumors sprang up as usual about the imminent liberation of the serfs, a minority of them believing that Napoleon would free them, while most thought the Tsar would reward them for fighting off the invaders.

During Alexander I's reign Russia for the first time achieved a position of international primacy, because of its decisive role in the undoing of Napoleon. Throughout the Napoleonic epoch and its aftermath, Russia, despite her sustained and savage defeats, occupied a focal position. Alexander's public gifts gave him the nickname of the Blessed. During his reign, extensive new territories fell to the Russian crown: Finland, Bessarabia, and spacious territories in Poland and the Caucasus were added to the vast, relatively uninhabited Empire, creating in the case of Finland and Poland additional centers of disaffection.

The War of 1812, made famous by the popularity of Tolstoy's *War and Peace*, had far less importance than it has been given. Napoleon's invasion lasted only six months, and it took the Grand Army a mere seven weeks to get out of the country.

There were still no elementary schools in Russia when Alexander's reign began, practically no state-sponsored secondary schools except military academies, and only three universities. An attempt was made to overhaul this skimpy educational system in 1803, but it collided with the same difficulties as all such previous attempts throughout the eighteenth century: the absence of funds, the profound mistrust of state-sponsored schools, and the dearth of teachers. The 1803 plan had pathetic results: in 1824 only some 4,465 pupils attended lower schools throughout the vast St. Petersburg region: enrollment in secondary school had risen from 5,600 in 1809 to 7,700 in 1825. There were only 820 students attending Moscow University in 1824, almost half the total number of students in Russia.

This was in sharp contrast with the private schools of the nobility, which emphasized such useful accomplishments as French and dancing. In 1824 there were over 2,000 students attending these private schools in the St. Petersburg region, as against the 450 in the state-sponsored secondary schools and the 51 in the University of St. Petersburg.

The simple fact that so many European peasants, however heavy their burdens, were free men who were not subject to corporal punishment was an arresting example of the abyss that separated Russia from the West even in a period of general agitation and breakdown. The contrast between the backwardness of the Russian masses and the military prowess of the Russian armies had a stimulating effect; when these young officers got back to Russia aflame with enthusiasm for the new ideas they had encountered, their renewed contact with the obscurantist regime of Arakcheyev and Alexander kindled the spark of political opposition.

European influence had a dual effect. The tiny minority influenced by liberal ideas was disappointed by the course of events after the settlement of the Napoleonic turmoil: the growth of the security police, the harshness of the censorship, the promotion of the military colonies—a peculiarly silly idea, both oppressive and futile, that was one of Alexander's quirks—as well as the general ascendancy of religiosity, both mystical and orthodox, in the Tsar's entourage, all gave the ardent liberal aristocrats a feeling of suffocation. In addition, the evolution of Alexander's Holy Alliance into an agency for the suppression of the liberty and national independence he had so often praised was inherently unpopular—Russian liberals found it both pointless and reprehensible for Russian troops to intervene in Spain and in Italy. Contrariwise, the more radical of the liberal aristocrats were excited by the upheavals that had become commonplace in Southern Europe as well as in Central and South America.

The Great Theatre (Bolshoi) of Saint Petersburg, lithograph by Gabriel Lory from an album published in 1799 in Russia under Paul I. The theatre was built by a French architect, Thomas de Thomon (1754–1813), in the French "Greek revival" style. It closely resembles the Odéon Théâtre in Paris. It was destroyed by fire in 1813.

The aristocratic opposition to the existing order came together in secret societies, a natural consequence of the concealment of strongly felt ideas. The opposition was expressed solely by the most aristocratic segment of society under the leadership of some of the greatest names in Russia. These secret societies, themselves the reflection of the great European current of thought aimed at "reaction," with parallels in the Italian *Carbonari*, the French *charbonnerie*, and the German *Tugendbund*, had a specific political character; some aristocrats even accepted the assassination of the Tsar as a means to their goal. These societies were in sharp contrast with the somewhat dreamily humanitarian Masonic Lodges that after a long period of suppression under Catherine the Great and Paul I had returned to Russia under Alexander I.

Alexander I, Tsar from 1801–1825, brought up by his grandmother Catherine the Great and a Swiss tutor, La Harpe, was gentle, charming and unstable. Vague liberal impulses marked the first years of his reign, but the last decade saw a return to reaction and bigotry. Engraving by Theodore Wright of a portrait by G. Dawe.

The Allies enter Paris, March 31, 1814. After Napoleon was defeated, the leaders of the Coalition (Alexander of Russia, Francis of Austria, Frederick William of Prussia) and their troops entered the French capital. This German engraving shows them riding by the Porte St. Martin, causing considerable emotion among the on-lookers.

The aristocratic mutineers had any number of reasons for disaffection: the corruption of the courts, the deplorable condition of the armed forces, to which as officers they were particularly sensitive, the abysmally low salaries of government officials and the resulting corruption, the savage conditions in the packed prisons, the economic stagnation, and the staggering burden of taxation, which oppressed all strata of the population, including the nobility. Above all, the condition of the peasantry was particularly upsetting to liberal Russians, who saw in the reform of serfdom not merely the fulfillment of abstract considerations of compassion but the furthering of their self-interest.

The general malaise was doubtless heightened by the widespread impression made by Alexander's personal brand of liberalism. There was an inherent tendency toward action in the theoretical liberalism of eighteenth-century Russia; Alexander's liking for constitutional government and detestation of serfdom were taken seriously in aristocratic and military circles. For that matter something had actually been done about it—constitutions had really been given Finland and Poland; there was perennial hope for a constitutional reform in Russia itself.

In December 1825 all these factors culminated in an insurrection caused by an attitude based on principle in contrast with the play of selfish interests. The aristocratic enterprise was halted instantly.

Only a handful of people were involved in the preparations, but they were in a state of hopeless disagreement on all practical points, and also split from the very outset into factions with basically different views. The great aristocrats and Guards officers from Petersburg, while agreeing that representative government and the emancipation of the serfs would be good things, were entirely in favor of property rights. They leaned toward a constitutional monarchy. The lesser nobles were far more radical. Paul Pestel, for instance, a founder of the Union of Salvation, was a republican: he envisaged a centralized, egalitarian, and democratic republic that would exclude all privileges arising out of status or wealth. He was also a Great Russian expansionist: he wanted to expel the Jews from Russia wholesale and conquer various territories still inhabited by Mongols. Prince Trubetskoy, on the other hand, thought the dynasty could be retained by forcing it to grant a few reforms. It was the inherent irreconcilability between these differing aims that doubtless explains its slovenly preparations. It was a complete fiasco.

Alexander's unexpected death in November 1825 forced the conspirators to advance the agreed-upon date. Alexander's death and the attendant uncertainty about the succession were a great opportunity for the conspirators, but all they could demonstrate was their unripeness. Trubetskoy's primary anxiety was to forestall popular intervention; he believed the insurrection had to be kept strictly within the bounds of an action by the armed forces closely controlled by their officers. He actually wanted an orderly upheaval. But, there was no question of any solidarity between the junior officers and the soldiery.

The fiasco was grotesque. Trubetskoy vanished from the Senate square, where the actual seizure of power was to take place, and Prince Eugene Obolensky, who took charge, had no idea what orders to give. Everyone stood around doing nothing, while government troops under the personal command of Nicholas, who had succeeded his brother Alexander, thronged into the square and the adjacent streets. The insurgents, though listless and unfed, refused to surrender; since their resistance was encouraged by a great many civilians who mingled with them and occasionally attacked the government troops with stones and logs, Nicholas decided on firmer action to forestall the transformation of the army mutiny into a popular rebellion. A few field guns were brought up; after the third volley, the insurgents were routed. By the time darkness set in, the Senate square was cleared except for seventy or eighty corpses, including some civilians.

The Decembrist revolt was futile. On the one hand, the people were utterly uninvolved, with no social group between the peasantry and the aristocracy-bureaucracy to provide the pseudorevolt with any social support. On the other hand, the revolt could not have been successful in the manner of the traditional palace revolutions because its makers had gone beyond such considerations, though not far enough. They tried to ideologize and socialize a mutiny in an ambience that had no foundations for it. Fundamentally, they represented only themselves, but since their education had projected them beyond the sphere of vulgar egotistic or cliquish ambitions and provided them with an arsenal of ideas, they failed to see through these ideas to the brute fact that socially they were in a void. They were in effect championing a nation that had never heard of them, nor could have.

In fact, if the insurgents had been more practical, the Decembrist enterprise might have produced an altogether different result. It was doubtless a case in which a practicable scheme was wrecked by its executers.

Despite the lackadaisical, inept, and to some extent cowardly character of the Decembrist uprising, it became a symbol for future generations of dissident Russians. It is true that the crushing of the insurrection, itself, for a time pulverized Russian liberal thought. Since the Decembrists had no desire to undo the existing order, they had no motive to sustain a revolutionary attitude. Most of the former liberals melted back into their milieu. Some members of the secret societies who had escaped Siberia covered themselves with distinction in the service of Nicholas; the exceptions, whose personal

101

convictions made such surrender impossible, thrust themselves into what was to become the underground.

The fact is that while the secret societies were eliminated as a result of the Decembrist failure, the conditions that had spawned them continued and kept their ideals alive. These ideals were a negative reflection of the various imbalances in Russia; their survival was ensured by the failure of the regime to right them.

Perhaps one of the chief effects of the Decembrist mutiny was its reinforcement of the repressive party in court circles. The dilemma facing authority in a situation of disaffection may be said to be universal: it is bound to turn toward either mollification or repression.

Nicholas, a drillmaster like his predecessors, was profoundly moved by the abortive mutiny. It remained a constant preoccupation of his, all the more so because it had involved the Guards, the flower of the army he regarded as the bulwark of the autocracy. He showed a keen interest in the Decembrists he had exiled to Siberia; even more, he was far from blind to the cause of their rebelliousness. Indeed, Nicholas was quite aware throughout his life of the necessity of some kind of reform, even though nothing was ever attempted during his reign. His attitude toward the master institution, serfdom, a suppurating wound in Russian society, sums up the dilemma: "There is no doubt that in its present form serfdom is a flagrant evil everyone is aware of, yet to attempt to remedy it now would be, of course, an evil still more disastrous."

The twenty-year reign of Nicholas I saw absolutism at its apogee. He had received a good education which, like Alexander's, ended at age seventeen, but he showed no interest in such things as political economy and government, subjects he sneered at as "abstractions." His chief interest was warfare, particularly military engineer in Nicholas gave the classical principle of Russian autocracy a slight twist of his own by emphasizing dynastic and religious elements, the supreme virtue of duty and discipline, and national tradition. His view of the state was essentially that of a smoothly running regiment, based on a detailed hierarchy, rigid specification of duties, and the unquestionable authority of the head. This lucid outlook was summed up by his Minister of Eduction, Uvarov, in a formula that was to become famous: "Orthodoxy, autocracy, and nationality." (There is reason to believe the slightly ambiguous final word of the formula was actually a euphemism tactfully substituted for the more down-right—and accurate—word, *serfdom.*)

In education this slogan meant that the existing order had to be preserved by eliminating subversive, i.e., liberal, influences. The goal of the authorities was to discourage students from studying anything beyond their station and to concentrate in the government's hands the control of all intellectual life. But the authorities were, inevitably, disappointed. In fact, Nicholas', regime somehow coincided with one of the greatest bursts of literacy as well as of intellectual activity. Not only were some of the greatest Russian literary masterpieces produced, but the seeds of almost the whole subsequent cultural development were contained in the geyser of creativity that burst out in the intellectual vanguard, constricted though it was.

Nicholas had close ties to the Hohenzollerns: at the age of twenty-seven he married King Frederick William III's daughter, sister of the future King Frederick William IV, and had seven children by her. He admired his father-in-law enormously, especially since the Prussian monarchy was an ideal of his. It was during Nicholas' reign that Russia, which had always aped one European country or another, turned its face toward Germany. In Peter the Great's time, advanced Russians chiefly admired techniques and the economic life as exemplified by Holland, Germany, and Sweden; France had been the magnet for the elegant thinkers of the eighteenth century; and England had a short period of tutorship after 1815, when the utilitarians, the Byronic movement, and the economists were looked up to. During Nicholas' reign Germany became once again a lodestone for the official classes because of her absolutism and bureaucratic organization, while at the other pole the intellectuals looked to her for philosophy and rounded *Weltanschaungen.*

German blood poured into the upper classes and the ruling dynasty itself. Germans had first become prominent in Russia because of Peter's personal taste for ability and accuracy, and in mass terms through his Baltic acquisitions, which had a broad upper segment of German landowners and townspeople. The ruling dynasty itself was completely submerged in German blood as a result of the union of Catherine the Great, a German princess, with Peter III, the son of Peter the Great's daughter Anne and the Duke of Holstein-Gottorp. It is curious to reflect that every Russian sovereign since Catherine the Great married a German, so that even if her son Paul was not Peter III's son but was, as is likely, the son of a lover of hers called Saltykov, the amount of Russian blood to be attributed to any Romanov after Catherine is infinitesimal. If Paul was indeed Peter III's son, the blood of Nicholas II, the last Tsar, was only $\frac{1}{128}$ Russian.

The cathedral of Saint Isaac of Dalmatia in what is now Leningrad is the fourth building of that name to be raised on the same spot. Peter the Great built the first ones in wood, then brick. Catherine the Great had Rinaldi replace these by a marble church with five cupolas. Alexander ordered a completely new cathedral to suit his taste for the monumental. Ricard de Montferrand won the competition for the commission, submitting drawings in the Chinese, Indian, Gothic and Byzantine style. His classical project with central dome was chosen. The cathedral was consecrated in 1858.

Serfdom was a knotty problem. The fact is that both peasants and landowners were being squeezed. The position of the aristocracy was only powerful from an external point of view. Though some 102,870 nobles owned about a third of the territory of Russia in 1859, the great majority of the landowners were impoverished. Of the above total, for instance, more than 75 percent was made up of estates of fewer than 100 male serfs, while those of over 500 male serfs made up only 3.6 percent. The landowners were heavily mortgaged; their debts kept running up, and it was quite common for them to be foreclosed.

The uneven pace of development that now began to be more and more marked in Russia also, oddly enough, brought about an increase in workers' wages. Industrialization, though still primitive, was progressing rapidly. The relative shortage of labor, due to serfdom and the prevalence of cottage industry, gave the workers a favorable position. Before the emancipation of the serfs, indeed, cottage industry could compete successfully with big industrial plants. Until the widespread use of machinery simple manufacturing processes could be done just as well by craftsmen as by big enterprises.

By 1860 the total number of industrial workers, accordingly, came to about 800,000, or a little more than 1 percent of the population, with servile labor accounting for about a third of the total. This was four times as many as there had been at the beginning of the century.

Mechanization began to become a substantial factor toward the end of the 1840s; it first made itself felt in textiles, where the technical processes were particularly adaptable to machinery.

As for education, it continued to be restricted to a small elite. Nevertheless, Russian scholarship was finally launched; in the first part of his reign, Nicholas had sent some gifted Russian students abroad to be trained as scholars. This created a core of professors who were often very distinguished and who were able to arouse the zeal of their abler students. But the number of students remained small: after an increase from 1,700 in 1825 to 4,600 in 1848, it declined to 3,600 in 1854, when Petersburg had only 379 and Moscow 1,061. Nicholas I, who remained hypersensitive to all signs of popular disaffection, turned against education because of the French revolution of 1848 and its European repercussions. In March 1848 officers of the Ministry of Education, including teachers, were forbidden to leave the country. The number of independent students was severely limited. The teaching of the constitutional law of European states, and even of philosophy, was stopped; logic and psychology were put in the hands of theological professors to make sure they fitted in with Orthodox views.

The standards of instruction in lower schools were exceptionally debased, to say nothing of the infinitesimal number of pupils involved. Literacy among the peasants was practically unknown: a peasant child could only attend informal classes where unqualified teachers, often retired soldiers with only glimmerings of literacy themselves, would teach the rudiments of reading and writing.

During Nicholas' reign, foreign policy revolved around a question that was considered to have become cardinal for Russia—the survival of the Ottoman Empire. The Russian attitude toward this question was expressed by Nicholas with a combination of insolence and ambiguity that exasperated the British and French and ultimately led to the Crimean War.

For Nicholas, the Crimean War was a crushing blow: not only did it mark the checkmate of the international diplomacy he had specialized in, but the army he had been so proud of was defeated.

The Crimean defeat had, as usual, an advantage. Because Russia was so humiliated and the autocracy's shortcomings were dramatically displayed, even conservatives were forced to face the necessity of a serious reform, a widespread feeling that came to a head after Nicholas's death in 1855 and the accession to the throne of his eldest son, Alexander II.

It is difficult to perceive the personal element in most of Alexander's behavior; like his uncle Alexander I, he remains immune to analysis. His practice of keeping people of irreconcilably opposed views simultaneously in office alone makes him elusive. Also, a curious streak of well-publicized sentimentality blurs the outlines of his of his character (during the war with Turkey in 1877–78 he proposed attending the wounded in person as a male nurse).

Alexander II is known as the Tsar-Emancipator, the inspirer of the Era of Great Reforms. His most far-reaching reform was the abolition of serfdom. After generations of social and individual malaise, this basic Russian institution was finally sloughed off. But it was done half-heartedly. The procedure was cumbersome and the results defective. The upshot was a regime of elusive complexity socially, administratively, and economically. While giving the peasants something, it did not give them enough to satisfy them; it left profound grievances. The event, indeed, satisfied no one, though it did, of course, transform society.

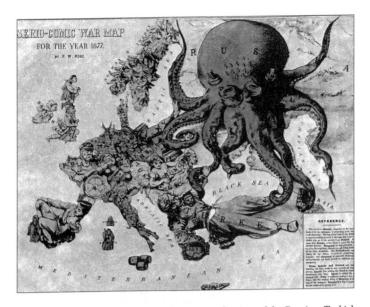

English political caricature map of Europe at the time of the Russian-Turkish war of 1877. Russia is shown as a great octopus ready to dismember prostrate Turkey, with the British Isles on their way to the rescue. Russia almost reached Constantinople, goal of her immemorial dreams, but was checked by the presence of the British fleet in the Sea of Marmora.

The reform was to take place in three stages, in the first of which, after the substitution of government agencies to perform the administrative functions formerly exercised by the noble landowners, the serfs were to be freed of their personal dependence on their masters. They were free to marry, own property, engage in commerce, and litigate. This was considered a temporary regime—though no time limit was laid down for it—after which land was supposed to be allotted to former serfs by a cumbersome system of redemption payments. The government handled the redemption debt, intending to make the serfs small farmers by capitalizing at 6 percent the yearly charges the peasant allotments were assessed at, and advancing to the landowners interest-bearing securities amounting to 75–80 percent of the total indemnification due them, the peasants usually providing the remainder. The government was supposed to be repaid by the peasants for the advances to the former owners. At first the peasants were given 49 years to repay the sum; the annual installments were supposed to come to the equivalent of the advance on each allotment, plus interest. Only after this obligation was settled could the serf regard himself as emancipated with a clear title to his allotment.

The 1861 reformers agreed that the former serfs should be given their homesteads and an "adequate" allotment of farming land. "Adequacy" is of course a slippery concept: the expedient was adopted that allotments worked by the serfs before the reform should be considered adequate. This was dubious since under serfdom the peasants had had to spend at least half their time laboring for their masters. An attempt was made to compensate for the known disparity in the size of the pre-reform holdings by splitting Russia up into zones, with maximum and minimum norms for each zone's allotments. The maximum varied from a little more than 32 acres to about 7½ acres; the minimum was one-third of the maximum. However, in most places the landowners were entitled to hold one-third (in some places one-half) of their arable land regardless of what this might do to the size of the allotment.

The difficulty of alleviating the plight of the peasants even after the reform was rooted in the general backwardness of the country, accentuated by the deadening influence of the village commune and the obtuseness of the government.

The peasants remained impoverished, with few prospects of betterment. A cliché for the general situation was "rural over-population," or conversely, "shortage of land." The oddity of this in such a vast, relatively uninhabited country is of course just another way of referring to the contrast between the number of people and the inadequate means of subsistence available, but in the minds of the peasants the feeling that it was the land that was somehow in short supply became a fixed idea. They came to look on the seizure of the lands held by the state and the nobility as the only cure for the "shortage of land," and of course as a primordial act of justice that should long since have been accomplished. This basic economic fact, combined with the bitterness caused by the execution of the 1861 reform, led to a tenacious belief in the inevitability of a "second emancipation."

The recurrent famines at home were in contrast with the rapid increase in Russian grain exports, which the building of railways promoted substantially. This was made possible not by any greater yields but, on the contrary, by extending the cultivated land still further. Here, too, the nobles were ineffi-cient: most of the profits were appropriated by middlemen.

Thus the nobility was badly squeezed in European Russia: it lost more than half its land between 1862 and 1911, chiefly to merchants, burghers, and well-to-do peasants. (A graphic description of this process, from the point of view of the nobility, is given in personal terms by Tolstoy in *Anna Karenina*.)

The reign of Alexander II marked the end of noble Russia. Gradually constricted by the newly evolving class of mer-chants, burghers, financiers, and industrialists brought into existence by the expansion of foreign trade, the construction of railways and of new ports, and the establishment of mines and factories, the nobility gradually began declining both economically and politically. It came to have little to depend on but the personal benevolence of the sovereign. The Russian nobility was finally eclipsed; aristocratic Russia had, in fact, become an external sheath under which new social forces gradually took shape.

Defective though the emancipation was, it nevertheless levelled to a large extent the dam that had been keeping the nineteenth century out of rural Russia. This newfound enthusiasm of the liberal and "penitent" nobility, to be sure, waned gradually as the country, once caught up in the millstream of Russia's Industrial Revolution, began to develop new turbulences, and as the intelligentsia, with more sharply defined and less exclusively humanitarian ideals, began to encompass the newly emerging conscious elements of the peasantry and working class.

For, an industrial proletariat was gradually forming. The gradual introduction of the industrial revolution to Russia was accompanied by abuses usual in every country: long hours, disagreeable working conditions, low wages, and the exploitation of women and children. In Russia, of course, such conditions were not noticeably different from the general situation, though they were sometimes worse. The working day was 12 hours as a rule, occasionally going as high as 18. Women and children as well as men commonly worked at night; workers were often crowded into dirty barracks, sleeping on the floor or on tiers of bare bunks.

Perhaps the cardinal factor in Russian economic progress was the great increase in railway construction mentioned above, again a result of the Crimean War, which had demonstrated the need of good communications for modern armies. In 1860, curiously enough, railways had been denounced as a pernicious luxury. In 1885 Russia had had less than 660 miles of railways, with another 330 added by 1860, when they began to boom. By 1885 mileage came to 21,780, a substantial increase despite Russia's vastness, though it left it with proportionately less railway mileage than any major country in Europe.

Externally speaking, Russia had made substantial achievements by the end of Alexander II's reign. Its foothold on the Pacific Ocean was consolidated; vast areas in Central Asia as well as the Near East were added to the realm. It had thrown off the restrictions of the Treaty of Paris, the seal of its defeat in the Crimean War, made Turkey powerless, and started a ferment among the Balkan Slavs. To be sure, this was no grandiose march of history but a rather casual tangle of events; ambitious bureaucrats and generals kept encumbering a country already far too large for its population, backward technically and culturally. With wastelands in Asia, men and money were squandered in pointless adventures in the Balkans. The 1877–78 war with Turkey, for instance, was wholly futile from any economic point of view. Russia had never had the slightest business interest in the impoverished Balkans, even more backward and peasant-bound than itself. The war resulted in a diplomatic defeat after a military victory chiefly because the British had been antagonized by feverish and futile Russian maneuverings in Central Asia; the British, overestimating Russian abilities, were nervous about India.

But it was, as we shall see, the formation of a new spiritual grouping, the "intelligentsia," that was to have a fateful effect on the world.

CHAPTER VII

THE INTELLIGENTSIA

European influences poured into Russia with the eighteenth century, but they were channelized into the nobility, which found itself elevated into a totally different world. This sharply focused and exclusive cultural impact split Russian society into basically two classes—the aristocrats and the plebeians, separated by a chasm that did not even begin to be spanned until the end of the eighteenth century.

They lived in different universes. Cities outside Moscow and St. Petersburg were no more than big villages. The merchants, with their beards and long cloaks, could scarcely be distinguished from the peasants. Even after becoming rich they did not abandon their old-fashioned manners; they did not become a bourgeoisie until almost into the twentieth century, when industrialization began remolding society at an ever increasing pace. The countryside itself reflected this contrast between the overwhelming sea of peasant humanity and the isolated islets of European manners. Monotonous fields and forests were studded by villages made up of squalid huts; at one end of the village would be found a splendid park, a huge mansion, probably with columns, and elegant people with works of art, libraries, and French tutors. A step away were the peasants, utterly unlike the aristocracy in looks, clothes, manners, and for that matter, language. Pious, respectful, sunk in folklore and a life of toil, both exhilarating and exhausting, the peasants remained untouched by the Western currents that had turned their masters into a different race.

The uneven evolution of Russia, its failure to develop its economic resources and the consequent delay in the formation of a modern spectrum of social categories, created a vacuum. As education developed, however slowly, and the liberal professions increased in numbers, this vacuum became the medium for a class known by the odd name of *intelligentsia,* a word long since incorporated into the international vocabulary.

The intelligentsia was never actually a social class in the sense of a fragment of society distinguished by characteristic roots, livelihoods, or manners. It was actually made up of all sorts of people from all sorts of groups: academic people, students, and lawyers were generally members of the intelligentsia; a great squire or a high functionary might or might not be, while a peasant would not, though his son, if he could become a teacher, might be. A good criterion might be its "world-outlook," an outlook that was rooted essentially in the notion that life was important, that ideas were important, and that the world should and doubtless could be changed.

This is, of course, a fundamentally religious view, and it may be that the intelligentsia grew from the deep roots of Russian mysticism. The secularization of Russian society effected by Peter the Great and even more by Catherine II had touched only the summit: when education began trickling out of the preserves of the aristocracy into the lives of commoners who, after 1857, began invading the universities, though in pathetically restricted numbers, the mystical element inherent in the people shot up to the surface at once and rapidly coagulated in a new and essentially messianic outlook. It engulfed the most influential stratum of Russian society, and in following the logic of its own development it created by the second half of the nineteenth century one of the most dedicated forces in history—the Russian revolutionary movement, which ultimately destroyed the Tsarist regime and for a time affected the world at large.

The Decembrist uprising of 1825 had been repressed with great vigor, but a ferment began to work that was to affect the newcomers to the universities. In the University of Moscow we can see its germ: the government, instead of finding a philosophy to justify autocracy, naively shut down the chair of philosophy on the theory that a study of it could lead to no good. This parochial Tsarist error had fateful consequences: the professor of physics undertook to quench the thirst of the student body for new ideas, and physics became exceptionally popular. People began bubbling with ideas; informal groups, united only by a general and often quite personal disaffection and by what Herzen called a "profound feeling of alienation from official Russia," leaped into being and spent their time discussing all sorts of scientific, philosophical, social, and political questions. This element of alienation was to be the imprint of the intelligentsia throughout its existence.

The influence of the French age of enlightenment, with its detached rationalism and empiricism, was still powerful, but it was gradually caught up with and overcome by German ideas. The tormented, uprooted Russian Hamlets who, floating about in a social no-man's land, with neither family, wealth, nor position, passionately longing to *believe* as well as to *know,* were revenging themselves on the elegant salon-learning of

Alexander Herzen (1812–1870) pioneer revolutionary agitator, novelist and journalist: founder of the newspaper "The Bell." Later the Populist movement grew out of his faith in the Russian peasantry as depository of Socialism. Photograph by the famous French photographer Nadar.

the Frenchified aristocracy. The skepticism, atheism, and liberalism of aristocratic salons since Catherine II gave way to a yearning for faith and a desire to change the world.

German thought was both a rejection of classical French rationalism and a way of bypassing the realities of the police state. A whole cluster of German philosophers, beginning with Schelling and going on to Kant, Fichte, and Hegel, came in turn to dominate the new intellectual universe. Hegel's influence was perhaps the most durable, doubtless because in its profound ambiguity the immense apparatus of Hegelian rhetoric has a splendidly mobile pivot: it can be turned in any desired direction. Radicals, conservatives, and all intervening shades of socio-political affiliation could find justification for anything they wanted in the *camera obscura* of Hegelian discourse.

But though German metaphysics was absorbed with passionate intensity—lifelong friendships were broken by a quibble over a Hegelian nuance—its intellectual remoteness gradually came to be chafed at.

Social studies began being emphasized in contrast with timeless philosophical lucubrations. France, in a different incarnation, was turned to again. The more extremist or radical thinkers began studying Russia itself, past or present, which in turn led to an avid absorption of French socialism—Saint-Simon, Fourier, Proudhon, Louis Blanc.

In the 1840s the tournament of opinion threw up two broad attitudes conventionally described as *Slavophilism* and *Westernism*. Both words are misleading.

The Westerners were basically humanitarians with a Russian tinge: they wanted to believe in a universal European culture and steep Russia in it so that it could transcend its parochial limitations and achieve world significance. "European culture" was of course a grab-bag of ingredients; since the Westerners had no clear-cut principles, they simply took their pick. Entirely heterogeneous in origin, they believed with varying degrees of emphasis in science, constitutional government, liberal values, and freedom of expression, and they were theoretically, though often tactfully, against serfdom. They also deplored the chasm between the Russian masses and the cultivated elite. They were far from committed to socialism; a leading Westerner, Granovsky, opposed it.

The Slavophiles were generally devoted to a glorification of the Russian national past—all quite imaginary. They looked on the West as decadent and enthralled by materialistic rationalism. They also tended to regard the Orthodox Church as the axis of the Russian people and its chief hope for the future.

They came chiefly from the landed aristocracy, and though conservative in the romantic sense were by no means in favor of official government policy, though there were of course points in common. Since they were particularly concerned with Russian Orthodoxy, they were hostile to the Church's *political* subservience, which had been a cardinal trait of Russian history. Politically, they were opposed to the Catholic Slav nations, which they regarded as traitors. For that matter they were also opposed to Ukrainian nationalism: they thought it disloyal to Great Russia, though this was because they regarded the Great Russian state as the incarnation of true Slavdom, and naturally called Ukrainian nationalism separatism.

Perhaps the most attractive and in some ways the most influential of the forerunners of the intelligentsia was Alexander Herzen (1812–1870), a novelist and journalist who

Fedotov: The Aristocrat's breakfast. 1849. This canvas, by a painter known for his scenes of everyday life in the prosperous classes, gives a good idea of what their surroundings looked like towards the end of Nicholas I's reign. The young man in informal morning attire would know French—the indispensable language for moving in polite society—play the piano, recite poetry, and dance gracefully. That would probably be the limit of his education, although as a member of the nobility or as the son of an official the university would be open to him. Nicholas had made study abroad practically impossible, and had limited the subjects to be taught at home. Cut off from the stimulation of foreign contacts, hedged in by the régime's intellectual restrictions in Russia, the young aristocrat no doubt spent much of his time losing more at gambling than he could afford. Ladies considering him as a son-in-law would inquire in French "How many souls (serfs) does he have?"

was the first of the "penitent gentry." Herzen was one of the principal channels in Russia for the somewhat vague though extraordinarily imaginative views of Saint-Simon. He had been given a conventional aristocratic education, largely under French influence, and at first he was attracted to some extent by Slavophilism. But when the two groups, which though vague about programs nevertheless represented differing casts of mind, fell out in 1844—the climax was occasioned, typically enough, by a series of lectures on the history of the Middle Ages—he struck out for himself, fusing a number of elements in a system of his own, a sort of synthesis of Westernism and Slavophilism that became known as Populism. It was based essentially on an idolization of the common people—i.e., the peasants—and looked forward to the institution of a form of agrarian socialism based on the village commune. Thus he retained the Slavophile adoration of the village commune as the source of all good things, while emphasizing its purely economic and organizational aspect and discarding the ethico-religious emphasis of the Slavophiles.

There was a completely matter-of-course interaction between literature and political activity. It is in fact this curious interweaving of the two that may be taken as the hallmark of Russian literature for most of the nineteenth century and later; it is certainly this aspect of it that has been accepted abroad as characteristic. Messianism was the significant element held in common by both Westerners and Slavophiles.

The earliest beginnings of modern Russian literature can be traced to the seventeenth century as an imitation of a Polish imitation of French models. But with the second quarter of the eighteenth century, the original source itself was turned to;

French classicism became the wellspring of Russian writing, chiefly through the work of the many-sided scholar and scientist Lomonosov (1711–1765). For decades after him, Russian literature was negligible: it is best understood as the digestion of the best of Western writing. Most of the writers were basically schoolmasters and translators who provided the channels for the new ideas and forms that came not only from France but from Germany and England. Russians were familiarized with various currents of German and English pre-Romantic literature and given new models for verse, which finally, in the nineteenth century, laid the foundations of Russian literature in its modern phase. This begins with French classical standards all over again; it was inaugurated by the publication of Pushkin's first book in 1820.

Early manuscript (1821) by the great Russian poet Alexander Pushkin: a page from his "Feast in Hell."

Pushkin, unquestionably the greatest Russian poet, indeed the Goethe and Dante of the Russian language, is both a literary ideal and a symbol of national culture. For Russians his immense charm is not in his being characteristically Russian, as foreigners conceive this, but in his universality, his "pan-humanity," as Dostoyevsky put it. Pushkin thought of himself as a Romantic, but his virtues were harmony and restraint: none of his effects is meant to startle. He is essentially a contained, delicate, classical poet.

Although Pushkin had an enormous influence on literary development, the swift growth of the messianically preoccupied intelligentsia bypassed him. After its brilliant classical efflorescence in the beginning of the nineteenth century—the epoch of classical poetry lasted scarcely more than a decade—Russian literature slipped into the mainstream of Russian moralizing.

The triumph of Russian messianism, in its two forms of Slavophilism and Westernizing radicalism, meant that after a half-generation of transition following the Golden Age of poetry, the basically dogmatic temperament of the committed intelligentsia suffused literature with purposiveness. Romanticism, which had merely been invoked during the brief classical period of Russian poetry, now made up the content of literature. German influences flooded the literate class, and the clash of political ideas overwhelmed literature. Art became the hand-maiden of other ideas.

The most characteristic effect in literature of the "two heads of Janus"—as Herzen called the Slavophile and radical currents of Russian idealism—was in the creation of the "natural school," a transition in which Gogol (1809–1852) may be considered the pivot.

Four Russian writers: from left to right, Krlyov, author of fables, Pushkin, and two other authors, Yukovsky and Gnedich; painting in the Tretyakov Gallery, Moscow.

Gogol's outlook was poetic; his first work was a product of a fantastic imagination quite indifferent to the social background that served as its springboard. It was essentially a lyrical caricature. But Belinsky found a social message in it; he explained to everyone just what Gogol had really meant or what he should have meant. Gogol himself was converted, and though he was not hostile at all to the social order, his choice of material, combined with the interpretation thrust on it by Belinsky and others, persuaded everyone that he was a social satirist. His admirers of 1845 thought him a model of realism.

With the surrender of poetry to prose as the core of Russian literature, the artistic serenity of Pushkin and his disciples was gone forever. The writer now sought some gripping world-truth; if he found anything solid he could cling to himself, he became a preacher. Gogol failed to find anything: for instance, in the sequel to his *Dead Souls,* the characters refused to be tailored to fit a moral purpose, whereupon he flung the manuscript into the fire.

Aside from content, as a literary genre Russian realism owes its forms to the French, especially Boileau, Molière, and La Fontaine, who were imitated and built on by a long line of Russian fable-writers culminating in the well-known rhymes of Krylov and Griboyedov, author of *Woe from Wit* (1825). Indeed, while the realism associated with Russian literature stems from the messianic commitment inspired by Belinsky and his followers, its language—primarily the absence of stylistic ornamentation—owes even more to the fine prose of the poets Pushkin and Lermontov. Pushkin's stories, to be sure, are pure action, and have none of the character-study that the Russian novel and theater have become famous for; but, he at least handed on his own form of realism in the classical spareness of his style.

The natural school gave rise to the Russian realistic novel, which, though many distinguished dramas were also written, wholly dominated Russian literature until well into the twentieth century. Gogol, in Belinsky's ferociously tendentious interpretation, became a model for later Russian novelists.

The dramatic effect of Russian novelists on world literature is surely due to their intense concentration on the portrayal of character. There is an absence of any distraction from "real" human beings by superficial storytelling. The converse of this, of course, is a certain narrative sluggishness and a general tendency toward the fusion of fiction and biography.

The indifference or hostility to style was doubtless a corollary of the real milieu Russian novelists chose to describe with painstaking precision. Between Gogol and the symbolists there was no attempt at linguistic adornment, which makes up so much of style in other literatures. Russians were preoccupied by a verisimilitude of detail bearing on the important problems of society as a whole. This was bound to forbid any purely stylistic excursions. The literary critics, whose role in Russia was disproportionate, could be relied on to remind an author of waywardness.

The preponderant foreign influence remained French. Dickens was very popular about 1845, but his influence was minor. Until 1917 France was to remain a deep source of Russian inspiration. George Sand was idolized; Balzac's following, though less extensive, was equally devoted. Tolstoy acknowledged the cardinal influence of Stendhal, most of all, of course, in the analytic method of establishing personality.

Turgeniev, born in 1818, was the first Russian novelist to fix Russian letters in the minds of foreigners. He was far better known than any other novelist of his generation except Tolstoy and Dostoyevsky; for a time his name outshone any other in Russia. He has since been outdistanced in world fame by perhaps the two best known novelists, Tolstoy and Dostoyevsky, with whom, together with Stendhal, the psychological novel of the nineteenth century reached its zenith.

Count Leo Tolstoy (1828–1910), photographed as an officer at Sebastopol during the disastrous Crimean war (1853–1856). Tolstoy was to use experiences gathered during this period in "War and Peace."

Both Tolstoy and Dostoyevsky were typical of Russian literature as a whole; they were increasingly preoccupied, indeed obsessed by what they considered the essential problems of life—death and God. The various threads in their writing can be disentangled only by disregarding the profound fusion of interest and execution in both of them. In Tolstoy especially we are obliged to endure his lifelong afflictions together with him. It is of course possible to discuss endlessly the ingredients of Tolstoy's art, but even when he was being most purely an artist, before his religious conversion around 1880, the whole of his outsize personality was at grips with the ultimate "reality" he was writing about. After his conversion, of course, his preoccupation became still more explicit, even didactic.

Tolstoy's career, though from a literary point of view it exemplifies the ethical nature of Russian writing, was socially unusual. Born in 1828, he received a purely aristocratic education: he had scarcely any contact with intellectuals at all before attending the university; even there, and for the rest of his life, he never had anything to do with them. Not only are the middle classes and their problems never referred to in his writing, but for all practical purposes they did not even exist for him. The only point of view he was aware of as even possible was his own, that of an aristocrat of independent means, and that of mankind at large, which for him boiled down to the peasants. Of all the Russian writers who became internationally celebrated, he was the least "literary": he was simply a gentleman. His intense nature and idiosyncrasies made him bored or irritated by society, but aside from his writing his life was that of a squire. His external interests were raising his family, farming his estates, and seeing friends of his own class; his artistic interests expressed themselves in stories about peasants and aristocratic families.

It is true that he gave all this up after his religious conversion, but he never became a mere writer. He turned into a prophet, exhorting the human race from the depths of his own discontent. With its patriarchal and profoundly aristocratic traits, Tolstoy's figure was an arresting contrast to the generally plebeian or middle-class atmosphere of Russian literary life. Indeed, his personal distinction, aside from his remarkable talents, was inextricably rooted in his aristocratic outlook: as a writer it made him unique.

Russian literature had a tremendous impact on the international public; but, with the death of Chekhov its great period, at least insofar as its world influence is concerned, was practically over. The great age of the novel, itself, ended about 1880; Dostoyevsky died in 1881, Turgeniev in 1883; Tolstoy's conversion about then also meant the subtraction of his talents from the novel and their application to his hortatory goals.

The great event, both political and social, of the latter part of the nineteenth century was, of course, the emancipation of the serfs. It was widely reflected in literature. In particular the landed aristocracy, which had produced the classical literature of the early part of the century, had been decaying on its estates or had floated off to join the evolving intelligentsia. Scarcely anyone but Tolstoy retained a specific class consciousness; nearly all writers and thinkers, even those such as Turgeniev who had patrician origins, became more or less uprooted. By the time of the emancipation, the gentry was completely overhauled: the middle layers were finished off by the pressure of the emancipation and its aftermath; the aristocracy proper was isolated.

Meanwhile, the intelligentsia, which had been in the grip of the two broad currents of Slavophilism and Westernizing radicalism, was being polarized still more sharply. The romantic Slavophilism of the early intelligentsia turned into Russian Pan-Slavism, which simply became a synonym for the ambitions of the Russian state. The sentimental theories formerly held about Slav kinship were exploited to provide the autocracy with pretexts for expansion. From the view that the Slavs as a whole were united by deep ties of culture and psychology, the Pan-Slavists, whose influence grew substantially after the national humiliation of the Crimean War, began to formulate a crude theory that it was the mission of Russia to liberate the Slavs from foreign yokes.

The theory, aside from encompassing irreconcilable differences about all conceivable details, was encumbered by insoluble riddles. For those Pan-Slavists who based their claims of Russia's historic mission on religious grounds, the disadvantage was that it excluded all Roman Catholic Slavs, such as the Poles, who were loathed by all Russian Pan-Slavists, as well as the Czechs and Croats, unless they recanted their Catholic "heresy," which was highly unlikely. Since by the end of 1906 all the Slavs in the world were thought to number some 150 million—of whom 70 percent were Greek Orthodox, 23 percent Roman Catholics, and the remainder either Uniats, dissidents, Protestants, or Muslims—this was a substantial loss for the religiously motivated wing of Pan-Slavism.

The less pious Pan-Slavists disregarded the religious issue and developed a quasi-ethnic basis for Slav unity: the cardinal factor in Slavdom's position in the world was the historic struggle between the Slavs and Western (i.e., German-Magyar) Europe. The conduct of this struggle had to depend on Russia, the only great Slav power.

It need hardly be pointed out that all such claims belong to mythology. This is of course very powerful, but in fact the Russians ultimately failed to achieve anything beyond adding one more element of confusion to the imbroglio of the First World War, from which Russia was to emerge so disastrously. On any rational plane, of course, the comparison with Germans and Italians was fatal: unlike them, the Slavic peoples had never developed any common culture but had simply evolved under the impact of cultures imported from various points abroad.

Dmitri Mendeleyev (1834–1907), chemist. After preparatory work in Russia and Paris, Mendeleyev studied oil in Pennsylvania and the Caucasus. Later he held a chair at the University of St. Petersburg. He wrote celebrated studies on oil and the compression of gas.

Ivan Pavlov (1849–1936), famous physiologist. Pavlov founded the Russian school of physiology. His main research concerned the work of the digestive glands. He was awarded the Nobel prize in 1904.

The Poles, Czechs, Croats, and Slovaks, for instance, had been molded entirely by Western Europe and Catholic influences. There is, in fact, no such thing as Slavic civilization in the sense of what the term means for French, Italians, or Germans; hence the opposition of Slavdom to the decadent West was literally senseless.

The interest taken by Russia in its Slavic brethren after the Crimean War was quite novel; beforehand it had been negligible. As for the Russian attempt to involve the Balkan Slavs in the schemes of the Russian state, not many of them were willing to exchange Austrians, Magyars, or even Turks for Russians. They were not encouraged by what had happened to Poland.

Pan-Slavism was not a genuine emotional focus as its more intellectual predecessor, Slavophilism, had been; it was a mere device of statecraft. Its basic significance lies in its political role; it became a rallying-point for the Pan-Russian agitation that preceded the First World War.

At the other end of the spectrum, the former Westernizing movement also began delineating itself far more sharply. The fusion between the educated elements of the middle and smaller gentry and the self-made intellectuals, in Russian the "men-of-all-ranks" who had somehow slipped into an education, formed a milieu that was to take its abstract ideas into the field of action.

An organized movement took up the ancient heritage of Russian rebelliousness. A sector of the intelligentsia broadened its messianic perspective to encompass the overthrow not merely of the political regime but of the whole of the social order. Simultaneously it organized, for the first time in history, a movement for the realization of this apocalyptic vision. This

133

movement ultimately swept the field and created a new society over the ruins of Tsarism.

To see the movement in perspective, let us glance at its formation.

CHAPTER VIII

DISSIDENCE ORGANIZED

The revolutionary movement carried disaffection to a logical extreme. Almost as soon as the intelligentsia became conscious of itself as a special group with an awareness of the contrast between Russia and Europe, a desire to do something about it began growing. Soon it took an organized form.

During the second quarter of the nineteenth century Russia, for the first time, developed an articulate group of people prepared to criticize the authorities—the foreshadowing of public opinion. Those vitally interested in reform were no longer a handful of people from the social elite, such as the Decembrist noblemen, but represented the plebeian classes. Despite all the efforts at censorship, journalism, literature, and even the theater reflected a state of uneasiness, however veiled, about social affairs. Initially, to be sure, the ferment was limited to the educated few.

In this quarter of the nineteenth century "official Russia" diverged from liberal opinion. Nicholas I began tightening the screws in reaction to the subversive currents agitating Europe toward the turbulent year of 1848. In 1847 Herzen, who had been optimistic about the possibility of working for his ideals in Russia, finally left for good. Having inherited a large fortune, he devoted himself to promoting his ideas.

Though Herzen had no objection in principle to revolutionary action, he thought everything necessary could stem far more appropriately from the Tsar. His special concern was social and economic reform, especially the abolition of serfdom, which at first he hailed enthusiastically.

But when the aftermath of the emancipation shifted the peasant question into a far more serious perspective, Herzen's influence declined. It is true that he gave the nascent revolutionary movement two of its most lasting slogans: in an editorial in Herzen's little journal, *The Bell*, [of July 1861] entitled "What Do the People Need?" his reply, rooted in his indignant rejection of the results of the emancipation program, was simple—"land and liberty." This motto became a rallying cry for generations.

A natural reaction to Nicholas I's authoritarianism was its transformation into its opposite. In the 1860s a mood was generated for which the word applied by Turgeniev to his famous hero, Bazarov—Nihilism—has become standard. The Nihilists denied all authority of whatever origin: not merely the state, family, and religion, but science as well, or at any rate absolute Science.

The Nihilists, after replacing the utopians of the 1840s, were succeeded in their turn by the practical revolutionaries. The sentimental philosophizing of the Fourierists yielded to a determination to change society as well as talk about it.

This determination did not bear fruit for a decade. Russia had no revolutionary movement at all during the 1850s: Herzen's *The Bell*, published abroad, was the only focus of subversion. But in the optimistic atmosphere surrounding the accession of Alexander II, the winds of radicalism began to blow.

Broadly speaking, the revolutionary movement was made up of two currents—Populism and Marxism. Populism was launched in a sense by Herzen, though his essentially humanitarian, social-reformist, perhaps sentimental views were swiftly out distanced by the anarchist terrorism interwoven with the fabric of the new movement. In addition to "Land and Liberty," his other rallying-cry, "Go to the people!" (an exhortation written in November 1861 to the students expelled from the universities in a general shut-down) remained magnetic for generations, perhaps because of its inchoate, indeed almost meaningless yet ardent pathos.

The Populist attempt to organize the peasants was based on the idea that they were intrinsically hostile to the official regime. The desire to "go to the people" did not mean, to be sure, that the people were available. The Populist movement, in fact, developed a terrorist wing that was far more notorious, and indeed effective, than any of its other elements, just because the people failed to respond to the fervent enthusiasm of the youths who found a goal for their idealism in the notion of inflaming the sodden, oppressed Russian masses with a broad vision of a new society.

Herzen was far too rhetorical and humanitarian for them. By 1865, when he transferred the printing press and editorial offices of *The Bell* to Geneva, the center of the new Russian emigration, it was obvious that he had been left far behind by the new developments. After 1863 the circulation of *The Bell*, never more than 3,000 copies in any case, slumped: it was suspended in 1867. Herzen, embittered and characteristically disillusioned, died in 1870.

The success of the Paris Commune of 1871 in surviving for several weeks was very encouraging to the "immediate action" groups among the revolutionaries. It influenced their attitudes both in the shake-up of 1905 and in the upheaval of 1917.

Michael Bakunin (1818–1876), son of a rich nobleman, had fabulous energy and temperament. He was a sort of one-man hurricane; from the age of twenty-five he was the eye of every tornado in Europe. A founder together with Marx of the International Workingman's Association of 1864—the "First International"—he soon broke with Marx and after many violent disputes was expelled from the International in 1872. He died as he was about to try launching a revolution in Italy.

The general structure of Populism, whose progress we have been tracing from Herzen's writings of the late 1840s and early 1850s through its elaboration ten or twenty years later by Chernyshevsky, Dobrolyubov, Nechayev, Tkachev, Lavrov, Bakunin, and others, rested on the following points: the Russian existing order, which was doomed and had to be overthrown by a socialist revolution, was different from that of other countries. It was this difference that permitted free-enterprise to be skipped over altogether and socialism to be embarked on directly. This conclusion was based on the assumption that a couple of specifically Russian institutions—the village commune and the associations of workmen and craftsmen *(artels)*—were in harmony with socialism; hence free-enterprise in Russia would be a step backward. The fraternal cooperation assumed to underlie these institutions was considered to derive from the character of the Russian peasants, collectively minded by instinct and therefore the authentic force behind the revolutionary movement.

Left: Many of the XIXth century revolutionaries were intellectuals with upper-class backgrounds. Prince Peter Kropotkin (1842–1921), who contributed vast sums to the revolutionary movement.

Center: Vissarion Belinsky (1810–1848), who used literary criticism as a vehicle to diffuse social theories of the intelligentsia. His messianic aspirations and "Western" leanings influenced a whole younger generation.

Right: Michael Bakunin (1818–1872), the father of revolutionary anarchy. Well-born, dynamic, Bakunin founded the First International with Marx. Portrait by the famous French photographer Nadar.

Perhaps just because its large-scale program was difficult to formulate, the practical echoes of Populism in ordinary life were far from trivial. A long series of revolutionary periodicals began appearing in Russia in the autumn of 1861 and went on until the 1917 upheaval. Secret societies of the modern kind, after Chernyshevsky's short-lived Young Russia, really began in 1862 with the establishment in Petersburg of *Land and Liberty*, the first important one, though it only lasted a couple of years. Chernyshevsky was in close contact with it. These were only the first organizational and propagandist attempts to arouse opposition to the official regime.

When women were barred from universities in 1863, as part of the official repression, Russian girls began flocking abroad, especially to Zurich, to be drenched in systematic propaganda, by now becoming dense enough to constitute an entire philosophy of life. It took the government a decade to see the results of this expatriation of able, idealistic young women. It finally issued an edict promising the opening of higher schools for women in Russia and ordering the students home by the end of 1873 on pain of exclusion from Russian schools and government employment. But though most of the Russian girls came back, it was only in order to participate in a mass propaganda campaign among the peasantry that the revolutionary groups had meanwhile decided on. It seemed as though the government's activities, as usual both too extreme and not extreme enough, could only help its enemies.

The movement "To the People" assumed an organizational character in the "crazy" summer of 1874. Thousands of young men and women, inflamed by optimistic reports that the countryside was about to explode, put on peasant clothing and invaded rural Russia. Some of them tried to set up fixed centers for agitation; others roved about preaching. But their ideas were so far removed from the peasants' experience that though they were sometimes listened to with approval, the strange crusade, watched in any case with great vigilance by the police, came to little. The revolutionaries were arrested in droves; the chief Petersburg organization was eliminated in the winter of 1874–75.

The failure of the attempt to appeal to the People directly and arouse its conscience stimulated the growth of terrorism. The young intellectuals, despairing of attracting the masses to their idealism, decided to fight the autocracy personally, in the name of the People to be sure.

In 1878 an organization was formed in Petersburg that revived the name of *Land and Liberty;* it embodied many terrorist principles. A new approach "To the People" was made in 1877–78; now the peasants were cajoled not by the mere preachings of individual idealists but by the revolutionists disguising themselves as important personages, such as storekeepers, trained workmen, and teachers. The peasants remained irremediably apathetic; the only people to pay attention to the movement in its revised form were the police; by 1879 the second crusade "To the People" had evaporated. Its failure accentuated the lethal idealism of the youth.

Sometimes, there was a peasant response. A peculiar charade was performed in the Province of Kiev in the style of an amusing anachronism. Some flexible revolutionaries talked a few thousand peasants into joining a clandestine organization sworn to the defense of the autocracy: the ringleaders wrote a bogus manifesto in the name of Alexander II giving all the land to the peasants and declaring the emancipation Acts of 1861 a forgery; they called on the peasants to organize in secret and free the shackled Tsar from the aristocratic and bureaucratic usurpers. This curious modern dress revival of a Pugachov drama was uncovered in 1877; about a thousand people were arrested. The spirited improvisation, however, had nothing to do with *Land and Liberty*.

Though *Land and Liberty* contained views that were both terrorist and purely educational, the difficulty of establishing effective contact with the peasantry weighted the balance in favor of terrorism, a trend that was strengthened by the celebrated case of Vera Zasulich.

An unsuccessful demonstration had been staged by *Land and Liberty* in December 1876 in Petersburg; the few dozen participants were roughly handled by the police, the leaders arrested, tried, and given long terms in jail. One of them, Bogolyubov, was flogged by General Trepov, Military Governor of Petersburg; the revolutionaries decided to protest by killing Trepov. Vera Zasulich, a twenty-nine-year-old aristocrat who knew neither Bogolyubov nor Trepov but was an active revolutionary who had been imprisoned for two years at the age of twenty, forestalled everyone by firing at and seriously wounding Trepov in 1878.

Her trial symbolized the general indictment of the regime: to the dismay of the authorities, she was quickly given a verdict of not guilty. A huge crowd in the courtroom and outside, including even higher bureaucrats, applauded in rapture. An attempt to arrest her again and set aside the verdict was checkmated; she was slipped secretly out of the country by friends and returned legally to Russia only after the 1905 amnesty.

The Zasulich trial shed some light on the mentality of the upper classes. In the struggle between the Tsarist autocracy and the revolutionaries, the wild applause that greeted

Zasulich's acquittal must be taken as a sign that the most solidly established stratum in Russian society was not sure of its moral position.

Political terror was immensely stimulated by the Zasulich case. A great many Populists were impressed by the popular endorsement of terrorism that was thought to be the significance of the verdict. Outrages on the persons of state officials, including, of course, policemen, became rife; logically enough, they led to an attempt on the life of the Tsar.

The issue of regicide divided *Land and Liberty*, which split up in October 1879 after Solovyov, one of its members, fired five shots at the Tsar and missed. Solovyov had used a party gun without authorization; on this the internal dissension came to a head, splitting the party into the *People's Will* and the *Total Partition*, the latter led by the founder of Russian Marxism, George Plekhanov.

Though the *People's Will* used a conventional humane vocabulary revolving around socialism, faith in the people, the overthrow of autocracy, and democratic representation, in fact it concentrated solely on the killing of the Tsar, which after seven attempts it finally succeeded in accomplishing in March 1881. Their preparations testified to boundless zeal, painstaking diligence, and great personal daring, all in the name of an ideal.

A final spasm of activity was the abortive attempt in 1887 to kill Alexander III. One of the five young men executed for the attempt was Lenin's older brother, Alexander Ulyanov.

The Populist wing of the revolutionary movement underwent a crisis primarily because of the groundlessness of its two basic assumptions—the political effectiveness of terror, and the indispensable peasant leadership of the revolution. Its basic attitudes were to be inherited by the Social Revolutionary Party, which remained a factor in Russian life until shortly after the 1917 Bolshevik putsch. But toward the end of the nineteenth century the Marxist movement, which had already made substantial progress in Europe, began overshadowing Populism.

Marxism was much later in coming to Russia than Populism, though the first translation of *Das Kapital,* published in 1867, was the Russian version of 1869. Itself a form of idealism, Marxism nevertheless reflected an organic development, the emergence of an industrial proletariat.

Marxism in its Russian form may be broadly summed up as the contention that Russian history was a part of universal history. This meant that Russia had to pass through capitalism in order to reach the future socialist society, that neither the peasantry nor its characteristic institutions were conducive to socialism, in contrast with the proletariat, that terrorism must be abandoned, and that the main task of the revolutionary leaders was to create a disciplined working-class party to conduct Russia into the promised land.

This program diverged from Populism on fundamental points, of course, and since for a long time neither group had a mass base, the energies of a small number of intellectuals were expended in arguing with each other. From 1883 on, Marx and Engels were translated, adapted, pored over, commented on, and analyzed, in order to funnel everything they said into the historical conditions of Russia. By 1883–84 small groups of "scientific" socialists were formed, chiefly among university students. By 1887 *Das Kapital* was the most popular book among students.

144

But despite their hope that the motive force for the revolution was to be found in the nascent Russian working class, these early Marxist students had very tenuous connections with the workers or none at all. The great strikes, for instance, that broke out in the 1880s and early 1890s owed nothing to ideology—they were due primarily to economic grievances, the growing pains of Russian free-enterprise. The police and troops found their repression a simple matter. In the beginning, Russian Marxism was just as detached an intellectual effort as the other products of the intelligentsia: it was essentially a literary discussion group.

Marxism's faith in the development of the objective forces of society protected it from the Tsarist censors: the notion developed in the early eighties that Marxists were actually friendly to capitalism because of their conviction that Russia had to develop a bourgeois society. To Marxists, the capitalist system was *bound* to succeed feudalism, just as it was *bound* to precede socialism; consequently some orthodox Marxists favored capitalism to such an extent that in the calamitous famine of 1891–92 they were against helping the peasants for fear of hindering the growth of capitalism.

In its early days Russian Marxism was also sometimes identified with the Manchester School of economics: this was why for some time the Tsarist government tolerated what was called "legal Marxism." Aided by its antiterrorist character, Marxism in this form could be expressed in the legal Russian press. Until the outbreak of the First World War there was, in addition to an illegal branch of Marxism, a legal one adhered to by many of the new class of business managers and engineers produced by the growing industrialization of Russia.

Until the middle of the 1890s, Marxism was a matter of polemicizing against Populists, not much more: factories and workshops were still too remote. About 1895 the term *Social-Democrat,* already current in Germany, began to be used for Russian Marxism, to distinguish it from terrorist or anarchist opinion by virtue of its theory of social development. 1895 is perhaps best taken as the starting point of the movement that in a little more than twenty years was to find itself at the helm of the Russian state.

Some twenty Marxist discussion and literary coteries in the Petersburg area, under the leadership of Lenin (born Vladimir Ulyanov) and Martov (born Julius Tsederbaum) fused into the *Fighting Union for the Liberation of the Working Class.* Shifting for Union's emphasis to unambiguous agitation among the working class rank-and-file, it combined discussion with practical activity. Moscow and other industrial centers followed suit, and by the end of the century the Marxist movement, though in size still negligible, was a real factor.

But it was still shapeless. A congress, or perhaps a symbolic congress—nine people!—met in Minsk in March 1898 to unify the movement. The nine participants were collared by the police out of hand. They had represented five local organizations and the Jewish *Bund,* a Social-Democratic organization of Jewish workers established the year before. The *Bund* was to play a stellar role in the revolutionary movement for years, but its relative importance declined as Marxism anchored itself in Russian society.

Russian Marxism, despite the scientific methodology it shared with other Marxist movements, was always splintered; perhaps the message of the scriptures was too elusive to be fathomed with precision. The great arch of deviation was studded with factions expressing every form of opinion from mild reformism to the narrowest views of the Dictatorship of the Proletariat. Russian Social-Democracy was always steeped in the most venomous, implacable, extravagantly expressed factional struggle, to the natural accompaniment of denunciations, splits, and excommunications. It would be a hopeless endeavor even to begin to indicate the range of groupings and regroupings that took place, even after the "unification" that finally articulated the movement.

An early—and decisive—grouping had produced a newspaper, *Iskra* ("The Spark"), that first appeared in Stuttgart in December 1900. The editorial board was made up of Lenin, Martov, Potresov, Plekhanov, Axelrod, and Vera Zasulich, the last three of whom were in exile. This initial attempt at unity was succeeded by the emergence of the Russian Social-Democratic Party at the Second Party Congress, the real founding congress, which met in 1903 with a joint program representing twenty-six constituent organizations.

But the program, though adhered to formally by the major groups until after 1917, contained enough ambiguities to allow the factional strife characteristic of the movement to go on even within the framework of a single party. The program was really twofold—maximum and minimum. The maximum program had to do with the ultimate goals of the Social-Democracy—the abolition of capitalism and the establishment via a revolution of a new socialist society under the Dictatorship of the Proletariat. The minimum program dealt with the immediate tactics of the Party and its structure: the overthrow of the Tsarist autocracy, the establishment of a democratic republic, and the eight-hour day; also, the restitution to the peasants of the land they were thought to have been deprived of by the

147

emancipation of 1861. The charter of the Party laid down the conditions for membership and the framework and reciprocal relations of Party agencies. The basic organs were the Central Committee, the council (dropped a couple of years later), and the editorial board of *The Spark,* now the Party's official organ.

It was the staffing of the Party agencies and the general attitude toward Party membership that led to a cleavage in the Party that far surpassed all other factional struggles and was never, indeed, bridged over. Lenin's group had managed to elect its candidates to the editorial board of *The Spark,* and the Martov group had refused to take part in any further relations to or accept a representation in the Party's basic agencies. At this particular moment, among this handful of individuals, Lenin happened to have a majority, on the basis of which his group were called *Majoritarians*—in Russian, Bolsheviks. The converse referred to the Mensheviks headed by Martov. With this inconspicuous beginning these names became fixed by history.

What must seem curious to us is that the profundity of the cleavage, which in the light of past and present history seems to us a matter of course, was unnoticed by any of the participants in the war of words that went on relentlessly in the mini-universe of the Russian Marxist emigres.

The differences between Bolsheviks and Mensheviks were never really formulated. Broadly speaking, Lenin was distinguished by an organizational preoccupation: he wanted the Party to consist of people whose lives were completely taken up by the revolution—a group of professional revolutionaries. The Mensheviks were satisfied with a much looser concept of "sympathy" with the revolution: they were willing to accept anyone who supported the movement intellectually.

The Bolsheviks were for the caucus as the spearhead of the proletarian dictatorship, the Mensheviks for the mass meeting.

Still more broadly, this organizational concept was itself the reflection of a more general view of the dynamics of planned upheaval: all Marxists considered socialism impossible without the establishment of an economy of abundance based on a society with the requisite culture and technological competence to undertake the industrialization that was the only thing that could make it work. They thought such a society could be brought into existence only through capitalist evolution, which would enable the working class to become mature enough to play its role as the midwife of the new society.

The Bolsheviks, however, thought that the Social-Democracy itself could accelerate this historic process and was indeed the sole channel for the revolutionary education of the proletariat. They conceived of their own organizational activity as a sharpened application of "consciousness," i.e., leadership. Just as Marx had reserved a special place for "Philosophy"— intellectuals with the right ideas, or, more precisely, himself—as the guide required even by the cosmic surge of History, so the Bolsheviks emphasized the indispensability of the right party—Lenin's.

Yet none of this was grasped at the time. Indeed, there was no place, properly speaking, for the individual at all in the Marxist schema, in which impersonal forces were thought to be working themselves out independently of human desires. Marxists merely thought they had a Great Key to history; it was the powers of comprehension inherent in "Philosophy," according to Marx, that gave it its special role. His schema, infused with "inevitability," could not be altered by human will.

149

On January 22, 1905, Father Gapon's followers advanced towards the Winter Palace carrying ikons and pictures of the Tsar. Their intentions were presumably peaceable; they hoped to read a petition to Nicholas II. The Tsar was away at the time. The Guards lost their nerves at the size of the crowd; firing directly at the unarmed procession, slashing at the foremost with their sabres, the Guards killed hundreds and wounded thousands. The event, known as "Bloody Sunday," touched off the 1905 revolution. This contemporary news drawing shows the Guards charging in front of the Admiralty, blocking the way to the Winter Palace.

This combination of general inevitability in the schema as a whole and the unconscious projections of personality no doubt underlay the extravagant factional wrangling and envenomed hairsplitting that filled the lives of the Russian Marxists.

In retrospect we may see that Lenin's distinguishing feature was willpower, doubtless derived from the unconscious assurance that in the expression of that willpower he was—in fact and beyond argument—identified with the working out of an ineluctable force of History. This injected a special element into the wranglings of the Social-Democratic movement, but since all forms of debate were necessarily expressed in scholastic language, Lenin's personal quality was never made manifest, especially since it was precisely this unspoken identification of himself with History that enabled him to be unostentatious, affable, and self-sacrificing. The practical consequences of Lenin's personality were not to be demonstrated until the autumn of 1917.

In 1900 Lenin was only thirty years old and merely one among other Social-Democratic leaders, far from the ikon he later became. In addition Populism and the romantic traditions of the *People's Will* revived somewhat and, toward the turn of the century, spurred on by the great famine of 1891–92, began growing once again with great vigor. The Social-Democrats still shared the field with the new Populist movement, known at the end of the 1890s as Social-Revolutionaries.

The Social-Revolutionary Party—its name designed to steer a course between the older Populism and the newer Social-Democracy—was formally established in the summer of 1900. In spite of itself, its program actually resembled that of the Social-Democracy; nevertheless most of the major

151

Social-Revolutionary groups both in Russia and abroad joined up by 1901. The differences between the S.R. Party (as it was usually referred to) and the Marxists were still great. The S.R.s believed that Russian capitalism was so weak that the collapse of the monarchy would lead automatically and at once to socialism; hence they supported cooperation with the liberal bourgeoisie against the autocracy. They also retained their faith in the peasantry as the motor of the revolution and were hostile to the concentrated bureaucratization they thought inherent in Marxism.

But the most dramatic aspect of the S.R.'s contrast with the Marxists lay in their belief in terror as a means of indoctrinating the public. This, in fact, was the only principle that tied together the otherwise loosely associated segments of the S.R. Party. The Social-Democrats, though they greeted the terrorist exploits of their rivals with a certain amount of glee, thought terror both pointless and pernicious.

In 1901 the Social-Revolutionaries devoted a specific segment of their organization to terror. From 1902 to 1907, when there was a slump in the revolutionary movement and the police were successful in catching most of the terrorists, a wave of S.R. atrocities swept the country. The central terrorist organization was extremely secret: its members carried their self-sacrificing zeal to a high pitch. Its membership was drawn from every section of society, including professional people and aristocrats. The best known leaders were Gershuni, Azev, and Boris Savinkov, the last of whom, under a pseudonym, was a well-known novelist and the protagonist of melodramatic exploits. (Churchill thought him the most fascinating man he had ever met.)

Azev's extraordinary role typified the complex relations between the security police and the revolutionaries. The heads of the security police were often highly sophisticated; they occasionally sympathized with the idealism of the revolutionary cause, and were fascinated by the revolutionaries themselves. Azev was simultaneously a terrorist and an agent of the security police. It would have been impossible to say whom he was *really* working for: he would occasionally organize a terrorist coup while hoodwinking his police contacts, while at other times he would ensure his credit with the police by denouncing his terrorist associates. He did this with such acumen and plausibility that he survived for years in spite of repeated accusations, dismissed by his comrades as calumny, a slander on the Party honor, etc. He was finally exposed incontrovertibly in 1908 by Burtsev, an emigré journalist and historian. The exposure of Azev was a major blow to political terrorism, which in any case had begun to wane.

The S.R. organization also followed a policy, entirely logical, of carrying out armed robberies for which "expropriations" was a handy euphemism. Regardless of the logic involved, however, the S.R.s were not easy in their minds about these robberies; they claimed they were trying to restrict these expropriations to government funds and not to kill anyone but police officers.

As opponents of terrorism, the Social-Democrats naturally could take a far less crass line, but Lenin himself was involved in a scandal by authorizing some "exes" of his own, successfully carried out by Stalin, among others. The Social-Democrats had no principle to advance in defense of these "exes";

Lenin either denied them vehemently or shifted into one of his incessant attacks on factional rivals.

The interaction between the police and the revolutionaries was so intense that not only were individual agents sometimes psychologically split about their roles, but on occasion even propaganda found its only audience among police spies. Some of Lenin's activities in exile consisted of delivering lectures; he would spend hours lecturing to tiny classes—perhaps four or five people—most of whom consisted of police spies conscientiously reporting back to headquarters.

The infiltration of the revolutionary organizations by police agents was given a characteristic defense later by Lenin and his sympathizers on the theory that the facts proved to have been stronger than political espionage and that the revolutionary organizations grew regardless of the role played in them by individual traitors.

The revolutionary movement was hampered for many years by hopeless wrangling and by its exiguous membership. Despite all their devotion, abundance of funds—the Bolsheviks also benefited by the openhandedness of rich patrons—and tireless energy, the revolutionaries remained alien to the peasantry and for a long time to the growing working class. At the beginning of 1905 a claim of a mere 8,000 members was made by the Bolsheviks; to be sure, such figures are inherently unreliable. The strength of the Bolsheviks was not, of course, derived from their dialectics but from the prevalent disaffection. It gave the propaganda of all revolutionary groups something to sharpen itself on.

It was not until 1917 that, in the case of the Bolsheviks at least, the importance was realized of the modern role of simplified propaganda wielded by a limber and well-articulated organization. Only now in fact can we see the significance of Bolshevik innovations—they were to engender a new world. In the Russia of the time there was no feeling that anything really serious was *happening*: the stability of the regime in a broad sense was unquestioned. However ardent the discussion of the new ideas, respectable society went its own way imbued with an attitude of composure essential for its peace of mind.

What was far more important, on the public horizon of the era, was the upswing in liberalism—the somewhat inchoate desire, generally associated with a constitution, for a softening of the monarchy. The famine years of 1891–92 that were such a stimulant to the Populist and Marxist movements also promoted liberal ideas.

To be sure, the huge camp between the autocracy and its enemies was filled by the bulk of educated and critical opinion, opposed to the state for its backwardness and arbitrary controls, but not to the point of advocating violent action.

The Rural Councils sustained this pacific, forward-looking movement, which was aimed, broadly speaking, at the installation of some form of popular representation in the central government and also at the creation of a central Rural Council administration. This would have had the effect of supplementing the cumbersome, high-handed central regime by a flexible, decentralized administration. The liberal sentiment that had suffered in the general movement of repression after the assassination of Alexander II cautiously began pushing ahead during the last decade of the nineteenth century and afterwards, invigorated by the ardor derived from the relief work done during the famine years of 1891–92. People were loath to return to the indolence of normal routine.

In addition, by the middle of the 1890s the so-called "Third Element," as the hired employees of the Rural Councils were called—teachers, doctors, nurses, veterinarians, statisticians, agronomists—played an increasingly effective role. This Third Element—the other two were officials of the crown and the elected members of the Rural Councils—was interested in the establishment of professional unions and in discussing issues of the broadest nature at conventions held with the tacit approval of the Rural Councils. The Third Element stemmed, of course, from the radical intelligentsia; many of them were linked to revolutionary groups. But as a body they reached beyond the framework of the Rural Councils proper and came in contact with other classes; the interest in professional unions, for instance, infected professional men outside the Rural Councils altogether.

Agriculture, in the wake of the defective emancipation of 1861, was still functioning poorly. There was another failure of crops in 1897–98 and in 1901; by the end of the century the defects of emancipation were unmistakable. The general agricultural stagnation and the progressive impoverishment of the peasants had their roots in the staggering taxes and in the paralysis due to the communal tenure of the land. Rural mutinies kept breaking out, illustrating the depressing statistics that accumulated about increasing arrears, meager crops, and debased living standards.

In addition, the working class began incubating a persistent malaise: the strikes of the 1890s went on increasing in number and scope. It was not so much their number: the manufacturing, mining, and metallurgical industries employed some

2,200,000 workers in the Russian Empire in 1900, while the strikers in the peak years of 1899 and 1903 numbered 97,000 and 87,000 respectively. It was the novelty of mass organized strikes that proved so disturbing, even though their grievances had not yet found a politically articulate channel.

Student agitation, which kept growing in importance, added a serious factor to the froth. Not only were living conditions still harsh for most students—an indication that the regime's attempts to confine higher education to the upper classes had in fact misfired—but the very juxtaposition of the poverty-stricken students to their elegant, wealthy fellows gave special point to the various levelling theories contending for attention. After a period of relative quiet in the 1880s, student agitation began taking on a more and more truculent character in the 1890s; in 1899 disorders flared up with exceptional violence for causes in themselves trivial. Assassinations carried out by Social-Revolutionary students became commonplace.

There was thus a fusion between the various kinds of opposition to the regime. Individuals with a variety of attitudes united in a common detestation of the *status quo;* though the remedies projected differed in accordance with outlook, the Tsarist fortress found itself besieged from all points in the compass.

Liberalism was established as an organized political force by the initiative of Paul Miliukov, a history professor, and P. B. Struve, author of the Social-Democratic manifesto of 1898, who had shifted over to the Right of the socialist movement. In 1902 they launched the first issue of *Liberation,* which advocated the overthrow of the autocracy and the establishment of a constitutional regime. The periodical, printed in Stuttgart, was smuggled into Russia.

It may be said that liberalism as an organized movement made its entry into Russian politics when the program of the Miliukov-Struve periodical, *Liberation*, was endorsed by the Union of Liberation, clandestinely launched at a Rural Council Conference in 1903 and formally organized in 1904. The Union, which had a network of local agencies, did not limit itself to coordinating the activities of the Rural Councils themselves but also managed to involve substantial numbers of intellectuals and professional men.

Thus lively forces in Russian society were in the midst of reshaping themselves beneath the crust of the autocracy, or rather alongside the obdurate element in the ruling stratum of the country, though life seemed normal on the official level.

CHAPTER IX

THE EXTINCTION OF TSARISM

The new sovereign, Alexander III, was unusually single-minded. He was indissolubly identified with the old formula "orthodoxy, autocracy, and nationality"; the element he emphasized was autocracy. He was profoundly influenced by Constantine Pobedonostsev (1837–1907), who tutored both him and his son, the future Nicholas II, and who was rightly considered the most powerful man in the state. Pobedonostsev's strategy, while defending the union of the common people and the throne on the one hand, systematically attacked the corrupt, self-serving bureaucracy, plus all proponents of constitutional reform, on the other.

Alexander III's regime became more oppressive on all the questions that had been agitating Russia. The press was gagged, the schools were thrown back to the regime of the 1830s, when children were supposed to be educated in terms of their social station, and "undesirable" elements, especially Jews, were excluded as far as possible from the educational system, which was forced into the straitjacket of intensified government supervision. Ethnic minorities, local languages, and dissenting religious sects were systematically persecuted (Pobedonostsev's letters to the Tsar overflowed with diatribes against Roman Catholics, Protestants, Jews, and Russian dissenters.) The treatment of the Jews was singularly harsh:

A forge in St. Petersburg at the end of the XIXth century. The industrial revolution arrived late in Russia but made rapid strides after the Crimean War. But while industry expanded, the condition of workers remained worse than in other European countries.

Alexander III himself had a special hatred of them based on a naïve acceptance of traditional anti-Semitism—the supposed Jewish responsibility for the Crucifixion. Not that anti-Semitism was confined to conservative and orthodox milieux: in the early 1880s the *People's Will* used anti-Jewish slogans.

In 1894, however, Nicholas II ascended a throne universally considered a rock of stability; to any superficial observer the country would have seemed tranquil. The police appeared to have suppressed all dissidence. The revolutionary movement was decapitated, its leaders exiled to Siberia and abroad.

The peasants were motionless; they had not even reacted to the great famine of 1891 in which thousands had perished. The Russian autocracy seemed to have lost nothing as it entered the twentieth century. It looked as tranquil at home as the international outlook seemed secure. Alexander III had been known as the "Tsar Peacemaker"; the international scene was calm. France had taken Germany's place as Russia's ally; relations with Great Britain were much more harmonious.

Then Tsarism was shaken up, for the first time, in the wake of the Russo-Japanese war that broke out in January 1904. Initially the war generated a wave of patriotism that overrode, for a time, the social frictions beneath the surface; but, as Russian forces, underequipped and outfought, were struck by one reverse after another, topped by the humiliating surrender of Port Arthur, the national opposition concerted its campaign against the autocracy.

A spectacular incident—"Bloody Sunday"—gave the mounting tension a focus. Underlying it was a convergence of police action and revolutionary enthusiasm. The incident began with a strike that broke out early in January 1905 in Petersburg and spread to some factories with tens of thousands of workers. The strike was directed by the so-called Assembly of Russian Workmen, a group organized and financed by the police themselves. Just as mutinies had been led in the name of the Tsar, so the police had done a certain amount of dabbling in setting up organizations professing concern with the interest of the working class. This one was headed by Father Gapon, a priest in the service of the police.

Whether or not Gapon was playing a role, he thought of appealing to the Tsar directly; he organized a parade of columns of workers flaunting a wide variety of grievances. The parade was peaceful; some of the marchers actually carried sacred ikons and portraits of the Tsar. But the demonstrators were stopped by cordons of troops and fired on when they refused to disperse. Official estimates listed some 130 killed and several hundred wounded. No doubt the casualties were much heavier.

The demonstration and its bloody sequel made a dramatic impression, out of all proportion to the number of casualties. The agitation of the Rural Councils and a variety of other bodies was intensified; in February the Grand Duke Sergius, the Tsar's uncle and brother-in-law, was assassinated in a coup planned by Savinkov under the protection of Azev.

The government reacted irresolutely: from now on nothing it did, including concessions made to liberal opinion, could catch up with the swelling disaffection that flowed in the two channels of conciliationist liberalism and revolutionary intransigence. The government felt itself forced to concede the principle of popular representation in an advisory assembly, but this was no longer enough to satisfy the liberals, who were now intent on securing a constituent assembly based on the commonplaces of political democracy in Western Europe—universal suffrage and a secret, direct, and equal ballot.

By May 1905, when the Russian fleet was annihilated by the Japanese in the straits of Tsushima, the domestic situation seemed hopeless. Agrarian upheavals, strikes, and political agitation by liberal and revolutionary groups (countered by the action of the autocracy's supporters, aimed particularly at the Jews) strained the situation to the breaking point.

A tardy concession in August 1905, which laid down the procedure to be followed for elections to the State Duma (the consultative assembly announced in February), was greeted

162

by open mockery. The definition of the franchise satisfied no one, conservative or liberal.

The universities were given a substantial degree of autonomy in an unexpected law of August 1905; the manner in which this was worked out against the background of the relentless pressure of public opinion transformed academic lecture audiences into debating assemblies, where speakers safe from police interference could erupt to their heart's content.

The political tension broke at last in the second half of September 1905 in a general strike of printers and bakers. A sympathetic strike was organized in Moscow by a union that was functioning in spite of no official recognition; it spread to the whole network in a few days, involving the telegraph and telephone services and halting almost the entire industrial plant.

The populace was deliriously excited: euphoric mobs roved about carrying red banners and revolutionary posters. Everything shut down—banks, shops, government offices, even pharmacies and hospitals. Newspapers, electricity, gas, and in some places water were all suspended; barricades were set up in a number of cities.

In October things came to a head: the Tsar signed a Manifesto (17 October) transforming Russia into a constitutional monarchy, and the "Soviet of Workers' Deputies," a by-product of the flood of oratory unloosed by the university autonomy decreed in August, met for the first time.

The Manifesto was devised by Witte, a former Minister of Finance recalled from semiretirement to conduct peace negotiations with Japan via the mediation of Theodore Roosevelt. It guaranteed basic civil liberties, promised to extend the franchise of the August law establishing the State Duma, and laid down an "immutable rule" that all laws had to have the sanction of the State Duma, which was also to exercise a control over crown appointees.

The concessions contained in the October Manifesto, a milestone in Russian political evolution, aroused the consternation of the conservatives and a certain amount of skepticism among the liberals. But the public reaction generally was one of unbridled enthusiasm. The conservative response took the familiar form of pogroms against the Jews; during the week after the signing of the October Manifesto, hundreds of pogroms ravaged small towns inside the Jewish Pale and outside, especially Kiev and Odessa.

The Petersburg Soviet disregarded the October Manifesto by carrying on with a general strike. There was, to be sure, a spontaneous and irresistible back-to-work movement following the Manifesto, but the Soviet had now become a revolutionary tribune; it proclaimed that the proletariat would never lay down its arms until the monarchy had been replaced by a democratic republic. The temporary governmental paralysis, plus the long-range calculations of Witte, who was biding his time, enabled the Soviet to act with a great deal of freedom: it handed out orders and carried on negotiations with the government. A partial amnesty granted a few days after the October Manifesto enabled many political exiles to return and resume their activities.

The revolutionary mood overflowed into the Russian hinterland: over 2,000 manor houses were burned or plundered and their owners killed or expelled.

The government finally pulled itself together; it proclaimed a state of emergency and sent off expeditions to suppress the riots. In November it arrested the whole Moscow headquarters of the Peasants' Union, a clandestine organization led by radical intellectuals, which had held its first conference in Moscow in August. Witte's calculations were bearing fruit.

Left: Count Sergius Witte (1849–1915) was born into the minor nobility. He first occupied a modest post as a railroad clerk. Later, in 1891, he activated the building of the Trans-Siberian railroad and became Minister of Communications the following year. As Minister of Finance he negotiated immense foreign loans and battled against the archaic structure of Russian economy. Opposed to the war with Japan, he negotiated the peace treaty after the Russian defeat. Nicholas II disliked him, but nevertheless made him Premier. As his last act, Witte obtained a manifesto from Nicholas creating a constitution.

Center: Peter Stolypin (1862–1911) able, lucid, was Minister of the Interior (1904), then Premier. A large landowner himself, he was responsible for agrarian reforms that so ameliorated the peasant situation that Lenin considered him a menace to the revolution. He antagonized the Empress by banishing Rasputin from St. Petersburg in 1911. The same year he was assassinated while attending the opera at Kiev with the Emperor.

Right: Constantine Pobedonostsev (1827–1907) rigid reactionary, close adviser to Alexander III and then to Nicholas II. He was a jurist, procurator of the Holy Synod, and against any form of parliamentary system or liberal thought. Pobedonostsev drafted Nicholas' accession speech, making it clear that the autocratic principle was to be upheld.

Now, in early December, as the tide of excitement ebbed and the hold of the Petersburg Soviet over its clientele slacked off, the government finally intervened. In a simple police action sit arrested all the leaders of the Soviet and dispersed it. A feeble attempt to replace it proved futile. The following month, January 1906, the government was in complete control again. Order had been restored.

One of the arrested Soviet leaders was Leon Trotsky, who at the age of twenty-six had played a stellar role as orator and writer. As Bronstein, son of a well-to-do Jewish farmer in the Ukraine, he had entered the revolutionary movement at the age of seventeen and had been exiled to Siberia and escaped. In exile he had been taken under Lenin's wing for a while; he had joined with Lenin at the 1903 Founding Congress in Brussels. But Trotsky could not, it seems, fit into Lenin's tight little entourage.

In the turmoil of 1905 Trotsky, under a number of pseudonyms, played an independent role; he was, indeed, the only Marxist to become prominent in the democratic arena of the Soviet, of which he was elected chairman. Together with fifteen other defendants from the Soviet, Trotsky was sentenced to Siberian exile for life. By March 1907 he had already escaped and made his way back to Petersburg, but, with the ebbtide in full flow, he emigrated. (He was to return a decade later.)

The Soviet lasted only fifty-two days; it made very little impression on the busy life of the capital. Nevertheless, the revolutionary mythology glamorized it at once; it was to be ikonized in 1917.

The 1905 disorders did not, in short, impair the Russian regime. The monarchy had survived intact; dissidence seemed quiescent.

The Russian imperial family photographed at Peterhof in August, 1901. The first four children were girls: Olga, Tatiana, Maria and Anastasia. In despair the superstitious Empress consulted all manner of quacks. Finally a son was born in 1904, but the parents soon learned he had inherited hemophilia through his mother.

Nicholas II, the last Tsar, was sadly outmatched by circumstances. To be sure, even a monarch more acute and with a more flexible character might have fallen short of the demands made by the upsets of the epoch. He was unable to cope with the inherited situation.

The Tsarina, whose mother was Princess Alice of England, had been brought up by her grandmother, Queen Victoria; Alice and Nicholas wrote to each other in English. After somewhat reluctantly embracing Russian Orthodoxy to marry Nicholas, she became an ardent devotee of her new religion: her mystical nature felt itself wholly fused with her conception of the union of the "People" with the crown, with a concomitantly virulent loathing of any curb on autocratic power. The Tsarina was both shy and sickly. Her health was impaired by the birth of four daughters, and the desire for an heir to the throne made her and Nicholas turn for advice to adventurers, faith-healers, and quacks. A longed-for heir to the throne was finally born in 1904; when the infant was only ten weeks old, the parents learned with grief that he had hemophilia, an incurable disease hereditary in the males of the House of Hesse but transmitted only through the mother.

The providential savior appealed to by the anguished mother was Rasputin, a semiliterate peasant from the Siberian wilderness. His powerful body, magnetic personality, and unintelligible talk—his "charisma"—had firmly anchored him in a coterie of Petersburg society neurotics. A characteristically Russian self-constituted religious teacher living by his wits on hand-outs from naive believers, Rasputin had an attractive combination of eroticism and mysticism: his creed was based on the logical assumption that forgiveness could only be accorded if there was something to forgive, i.e., the act

Born in Siberia, Rasputin arrived in St. Petersburg in 1903 where he was rapidly adopted by an aristocratic coterie imbued with mysticism and the occult. In November 1905 Nicholas II wrote in his diary: "We met a holy man, Gregory from the province of Tobolsk." This illiterate and lustful monk, with an intensely magnetic personality, dominated the Empress. Worry over her son's health had undermined her mental stability.

of sinning. He promised eternal salvation to believers who achieved true humility by way of sexual license.

The beginnings of parliamentary democracy laid in 1905 had had reservations that made its actual functioning difficult. Not only had the government dug in its heels, but the parties that emerged from the shake-up had proved equally rigid with respect to each other. Before 1905, after all, no political party had had any status: the Social-Democratic and Social-Revolutionary Parties that were to play a decisive role in the upheaval of 1917 were basically underground organizations.

The constitutional regime set up after 1905 established a spectrum of political parties that—at a casual glance—resembled their Western models. Opinion organized itself into groups that spread from left to right, beginning from what we should now consider the center. Extremist liberalism was represented by the Constitutional Democrats—known as Cadets, from their initials—a party, led by Miliukov, that had emerged from a campaign by the Rural Council groups. Its program was approved by the first and the second (January 1906) party congress; it naturally represented a compromise of contending views. The extremist demands for a democratic republic and a constituent assembly based on a direct and universal ballot were eliminated; the party as a whole came out for a constitutional monarchy, with the State Duma being given a full-fledged role in the establishment of the new constitution. The Cadets sponsored broad social and economic reforms, including the expropriation of great estates against fair indemnification.

The Tsar's daughters: Maria, Tatiana, Anastasia and Olga. Brought up in genteel seclusion, they had no reason to believe their quiet lives were to be shattered by future events.

The more conservative elements set up their own parties, the most important of which was the Octobrists, headed by A.I. Guchkov; it was founded in December 1905. Basing itself, as its name indicated, on the October Manifesto, it vigorously opposed the more far-reaching socio-economic demands of the Cadets, especially the expropriation of the big landowners. Conservative extremists joined in the Union of the Russian People.

With the shaping up of the parliamentary regime, the Rural Councils subsided as the expression of liberal opinion; until the abolition of the monarchy the new Russian parliament remained the arena of conventional politics.

The first two Dumas were far more radical than the regime had been counting on. In the First Duma, for instance, inaugurated 27 April 1906 (O.S.), though the peasantry was well represented and was counted on as a traditional bulwark of conservatism, the 200 peasant deputies (of a total of 500) turned out to be unexpectedly liberal; they took an inconveniently intractable line on all land questions.

This Duma was dominated by the Cadets, who were very disturbing to the conservative elements. Though the Duma represented 26 parties and 16 national groups, the Cadets had between 170 and 180 members and were generally supported by the Labor Group, which had over 100 members. The latter was made up of a merger of 10 groups that were even more liberal than the Cadets, especially about the land, but were not socialists or revolutionaries. The ethnic groups, such as the Poles, Ukrainians, and Letts, had about 60 to 70 members; they backed national autonomy and had a generally radical tinge. The Social-Democrats, now legally recognized, had a small separate faction. There were no conservative deputies at all.

The First Duma lasted only a few months. The very fact of its radical composition, as expressed in the demands it made in its program (adopted practically unanimously) insisting on universal suffrage, a one-chamber parliament, and a land reform based on expropriation, implied a rapid demise. By July it was dissolved.

The Second Duma, scheduled for 20 February 1907 (O.S.), was even more radical in composition than the first and just as short-lived; it lasted a little more than three months. Both Social-Democrats and Social-Revolutionaries had taken part in the elections (Lenin had been impressed by the First Duma's propaganda potential); the Second Duma had some 65 Social-Democrats and 34 S.R.s, while the Cadets fell to 92 and the Labor Group to 101.

The surprising radicalism of the first two Dumas pointed up a defect in the arithmetic underlying the theory of representation. The defect was rectified quite simply by reducing the number of deputies to be elected by industrial workers and increasing the landowners' ratio, and so a fairly conservative Third Duma was ensured.

Of the four Dumas Tsarism was destined to see, the Third Duma was the only one to complete its full term. Dominated by conservatives, it lasted from November 1907 to June 1912. The right-wing, moderate right-wing, and nationalist parties had about 150 members, as did the Octobrists. The Cadets had sunk to 53, and the Social-Democrats and the Labor Group had 14 each.

The last Duma—November 1912 to February 1917—was even more conservative: the right wing had 185 deputies, the

Octobrists 97, and the Cadets 58. The Social-Democrats kept their 14, while the Labor Group sank to 10.

Both the Third and Fourth Dumas were boycotted by the Social-Revolutionaries.

Perhaps the most distinguished newcomer to the government was Peter Stolypin (1862–1911), Minister of the Interior in the First Duma and later a powerful, able President of the Council of Ministers.

Stolypin intended to enable the peasants to own land independently of any other institution; he thought this would calm the countryside. He wanted to eradicate once and for all the village commune and thus launch a class of peasant proprietors. The basic part of a somewhat ramified scheme to accomplish this was embodied in a law of November 1906 giving an individual peasant the right, once he had secured the consent of two-thirds of the village assembly, to consolidate his scattered strips in the common fields into single plot, which from then on was to be private property in perpetuity.

Stolypin's legislation did not destroy the peasant commune all at once (in 1917 the great bulk of the peasantry were still being governed by it), but his agrarian reform laid the groundwork of a new peasant economy. By the outbreak of the 1914 war about a quarter of the peasant households in European Russia had transformed all their holdings into personal property.

Stolypin accompanied this far-sighted transformation of rural Russia by a ruthless repression of radical activity. There had been an upsurge of terrorism after the turbulent events of 1905; the Social-Revolutionaries had managed to arrange the assassination of almost 1,600 people in 1906, mostly officials of all grades, and more than 2,500 in 1907. This wave of murders reflected a general belief, shared by Lenin, that another armed revolt was in the offing.

In August 1906 the Maximalists, a newly formed S.R. group, blew up Stolypin's summer villa, killing thirty-two people, including the bomb-throwers, and injuring twenty-two, including Stolypin's son and daughter; he personally was unscratched. Though the S.R. Central Committee declined to take any credit for this particular outrage, the terrorist movement had frightened the regime; under Stolypin's energetic direction, the government reacted with brig. The security police were given immense latitude; the activities of the terrorists were countered by the lawbreaking of the security organs themselves. The extensive use of *agents provocateurs* directly involved the police in the most extravagant enterprises.

The wave of terrorism did not last long. The strength of the revolutionary movement at this time was altogether illusory. In 1907 the central S.R. organ was arrested and liquidated; by the end of the year almost all local groups had vanished. The activities of Ryss himself were finally noticed by his police sponsors, somewhat belatedly: he was hanged in 1908. The terrorists who escaped arrest fled abroad. By the end of 1907 the Central Committee of the S.R. Party, which after the amnesty of October 1905 had returned to Russia, was obliged to emigrate again. On top of this the exposure in 1908 of Azev's double-dealing, while highly embarrassing to the government, was even more so to the S.R. movement, which was nearly wrecked by the revelation. The Social-Democracy was also in a bad way. Rent by factional strife, its members arrested in droves, it almost broke up entirely. Even its fitful spurts of propaganda fell on stony ground. After Trotsky, Lenin emigrated in 1907, while Joseph Stalin, arrested in 1908, was deported to Siberia. By the spring of 1908 Russia was practically cleared of the whole of the revolutionary leadership.

The liberal movement was hard-pressed. The conservatives were winning, at all points, including the Rural Councils that had once seemed such promising arenas of agitation. The government, having abandoned its intention of keeping its hands off the parliamentary process, was lavishly providing right-wing organizations with secret funds.

Stolypin's Pan-Russian zeal led to an intensification of the nationalist element in his program. In practice nationalism—perhaps inevitably, considering the inherent blurriness of the concept—took the form of persecuting the various minorities of the Empire and of artificially ensuring the predominance of Russians in the quasirepresentative institutions imposed on the regime.

Russian was rammed down the throats of the minorities; it was made the language of instruction in the Ukraine, a special target of government ire. The regime made no secret of its hostility to the Ukrainian nationalist movement, which was suspected, doubtless rightly, of separatist tendencies, fortified by the autonomy accorded Ukrainians in the adjacent Austro-Hungarian provinces.

By Stolypin's standards his career might have seemed successful. During his regime the revolutionary forces reached their nadir, while his land-program, despite the failure of many conservatives to appreciate its significance—it was June 1910 before the program was passed by the Duma—had effected a comprehensive metamorphosis of rural Russia.

Stolypin was actually considered an enemy by the conservative elements in the government and at court; his boldness and energy, expressed with an arrogance due, no doubt, to his awareness of his superiority, kindled hostile intrigues whose success seemed ensured and that were forestalled, ironically enough, only by his assassination in September 1911.

Stolypin's death was an outcome of his condoning of the police network of double agents, spies, and *agents provocateurs.* His assassin, Dmitri Bogrov, was one of the revolutionaries on the police payroll.

Apart from the transformation of the peasant villages launched by Stolypin, other structural changes were being manifested. After 1905 the cooperative movement grew with great rapidity. The first Russian cooperatives, some forty years before, had made very little progress, but between 1905 and 1914 the membership of the cooperatives grew tenfold, increasing from less than 1 million to more than 10 million. While not impressive in absolute terms, the potentialities of this movement are obvious.

At the peak of Tsarist prosperity, before the war, the national income per capita was eight to ten times less than in the United States; this is understandable when it is recalled that in 1913 the number of people engaged in all nonagricultural pursuits—industry, commerce, transport—did not amount to more than one-seventeenth of the whole population, whereas in the United States over two people were engaged in industry for every person engaged in agriculture. Nevertheless there was a great industrial boom in Russia toward the end of the century; it achieved its unusual dimensions precisely because it took place within the framework of Russian backwardness.

The industrial expansion, particularly rapid from 1893 to 1899, slowed down in the first decade of the twentieth century; it speeded up again rom 1910 to 1913. During the 1890s, 15,000 miles of railway, including the Trans-Siberian, were built; this was the chief single cause of the business boom, which then slowed down because of the turmoil following the turn of the century. All in all, industrial production in Russia increased by roughly 100 percent between 1905 and the First World War.

But what was far more important was the character of the industry that sprang up. Russia's very lateness enabled her to dispense with the obsolescent features that hampered the capitalism of older industrial countries.

Thus, although agriculture and peasant life had not risen much beyond the level of the seventeenth century, Russian industry—in technique and structure—was well in the forefront of international capitalism. More important than absolute industrial growth was the density of the production process. This density, already noticeable in the first stages of Russian industrial development, became still more marked in the twenty-five years before the First World War.

A substantial element in the great industrial boom of this quarter century was the flow of money from abroad. By 1914 foreign companies owned about one-third of the total capital investment of Russian industry, and the great influx of foreign money accelerated the industrialization of the south. About a third of the investments came from France; England contributed 23 percent, Germany 20 percent, and Belgium 14 percent. France controlled almost 75 percent of Russia's output of coal and pig iron.

These aspects of Russian capitalism, confined as it was to a small sector of the population, and even more to the external world of socio-political affairs, are only one indication of the evolution of Russian society.

The cultural isolation of Russia from the West, which had lasted so long, was a thing of the past. The Russian educated classes were now on a level with their counterparts in other countries.

In spite of all obstacles, the number of students at higher schools had increased substantially. In the beginning of 1914 there were 67 higher schools numbering 90,000 students; this included some 13 women's institutions with 21,000 students. There were 36,000 students attending universities, 22,000 in the engineering and other technical schools and 10,000 in specialized institutions such as agricultural colleges.

The secondary schools also showed some progress, and the primary school system became an object of immense concern even to the conservative Third Duma, which with considerable success undertook a general reform. The general background of the problem, to be sure, remained rather depressing: in 1914, 49 percent of the children between ages eight and eleven did not go to school at all. In its broad outlines, the problem of illiteracy remained unsolved.

The industrial and political fevers of the turn of the century, as well as the increased freedom of the press after 1905, had a stimulating effect on literature and the arts. The realism Russian literature had become famous for during the 1860s and 1870s was sustained by a group whose leaders were Tolstoy, Gorky, Anton Chekhov (1860–1904), and Ivan Bunin (1870–1953). Tolstoy, in fact, loomed bulkier than ever, perhaps because of his religious conversion around 1880 and his ascetic repudiation of his purely literary writings. Having become a world sage, after working out a highly simplified form of Christianity that he himself considered primitive and that repudiated authority, violence, and all institutions, in short the whole fabric of accepted society, Tolstoy went on living on his estate in Yasnaya Polyana. His contradictory life filled him with growing revulsion, but he finally achieved a certain degree of spiritual consistency by attacking the Orthodox Church until the Holy Synod, which had shown great forbearance because of his name, eventually acknowledged a *de facto* situation and excommunicated him in 1901.

Ties with Western Europe were very close; upper-class children were habitually taught to speak French, German, and, somewhat less frequently, English. Foreign literature was widely read, and Russians flocked to all the capitals and resorts of Europe. By the end of the nineteenth century educated Russians were thoroughly europeanized.

Yet in another way this complete assimilation merely pointed up the profound chasm that has been referred to so often. Precisely because of these European influences, the upper classes were alien to the bulk of the country. The cosmopolitan attitudes streaming in from abroad were concentrated socially in the upper middle classes and territorially in the capital. Petersburg, with its splendid embankment and its baroque eighteenth- and nineteenth-century palaces constructed by Frenchmen and Italians, was entirely Westernized, physically and temperamentally: even the court and the bureaucracy were highly accessible to foreign influences. But the farther one got away from the capital, the farther one sank into a quagmire of life altogether alien to Western Europe. Even Moscow had a certain provincialism, and in the small

179

towns the imprint of the West began fading fast; in the remoter cities it was altogether absent. These were cities in name only, actually no more than peasant villages with no modern amenities to speak of. Indeed, 87 percent of the population, according to the 1897 census, lived in the countryside, and from the point of view of any Western European capital, the rural population might just as well have lived on Mars. In customs, way of life and thought, and even language, there was nothing in common between the peasants and the tiny educated class. Unless an aristocrat happened to take a personal interest in his land, the peasants and the upper class had no interests whatever in common.

Russia plummeted into the First World War, accordingly, with her ancient lopsidedness still embedded in her institutions. The backwardness of the immense majority and the cosmopolitanism of the upper class were radically out of balance. Russia's profound structural flaws were merely plastered over by her facade of monolithic placidity.

Tsarism had been no more than shaken up by the 1905 revolution. But the First World War had undreamed of consequences for Russia.

There is no need to discuss the causes of the First World War or for that matter the course of its development. Russia was involved in it with the same curious mixture of blindness and irresponsibility that characterized the actions of all the great powers. Europe had not had a war for so long, and the technological and organizational background of society had meanwhile changed so profoundly, that it proved impossible for even the most astute statesmen to assess an armed conflict involving the mobilization of millions of men. The very fabric of society, thought to be fissure-proof, was to be shredded by the war and its aftermath.

The economic and political structure of the Russian state was hopelessly outdistanced by the demands of a modern war. Russian leadership proved to be completely inadequate from both the military and the economic points of view. Having slipped into the maelstrom of a comprehensive conflict even more unprepared than the other great powers, Russia found itself short of armaments as well as of war aims.

Politically speaking, the war was supported, though with varying degrees of enthusiasm, by all parties in the government with the exception of the Bolshevik faction of the Social-Democratic Party, which took the intransigent position that the working class ought to fight against the domestic bourgeois and imperialist regime instead of against the enemy's armies. Though this attitude was eventually to help the Bolsheviks, at the time it simply meant the arrest of the five Bolshevik deputies who made up the legal, parliamentary section of the Bolshevik group and their exile to Eastern Siberia in 1915.

One of the major atmospheric elements, so to speak, leading up to the 1917 revolution was Rasputin's towering role. In the topmost circles, Rasputin's power soon became so disturbing that a plot was set afoot to get rid of him. He was assassinated in the palace of Prince Yusupov in December 1916; no action was taken against the assassins, who included a nephew of the Tsar as well as Yusupov himself.

The crumbling of national morale that led to the events of 1917 took place only gradually. A patriotic fervor swept the capital in the summer of 1914, as indeed it swept every capital that went to war; the fervor was shared by every social

Rasputin a few weeks before his assassination, surrounded by his court.

group. Huge crowds collected to express their dislike of Germans and Austrians, the mobilization went off smoothly, and the strike movement that in the summer of 1914 had set a record since 1905–6 simply evaporated.

As labor felt the pinch, it began striking. In 1915 more than a thousand strikes took place, involving more than half a million workers. In 1916 there were 1,400 strikes involving more than a million, and the strike movement kept mounting in January and February 1917. These wartime strikes, though somewhat below the figures for the first half-year of 1914 (when the strikes had been, moreover, partly political), were quite spontaneous; they had nothing to do with political perspectives or trade union leadership, except for the class-conscious, relatively highly paid metal-workers. As for the peasants, though economically they were better off than the industrial working class, it was they who had to bear the brunt of the staggering war casualties, which for the First World War amounted, on the Russian side, to more than 7 million men, the bulk of whom, in harmony with the representative quality of a conscript army, were peasants.

It was primarily the defeatist mood of the peasantry and industrial working class that was to undo the Tsarist regime.

No revolutionary leader was in Russia. Lenin was in Switzerland. Trotsky had made his way to New York after being expelled from one European country after another. Though the revolutionary movement had been decapitated, thousands of its members and sympathizers were scattered throughout the army and the wartime agencies and factories, but their propaganda was limited: there was no question of revolution.

The capital was completely calm the week before 23 February (Old Style). The excitement caused by Rasputin's assassination had died down completely during the first few weeks of 1917.

All at once some riots broke out. They seem to have begun among irritated housewives queuing up in front of food shops, spread with incomprehensible rapidity to the working-class suburbs and then flowed back through the main streets and squares of the capital. There was no violence; no hostility was shown by the police and troops; the city authorities were not alarmed.

At some point it became apparent that orders given to troops to stop unarmed demonstrators from proceeding along streets or over bridges could not be carried out. When a commanding officer gives an order that is not carried out and he cannot punish anyone for it, military dicipline is at an end.

The absence of authority was noticed suddenly—embodied most dramatically in the simple fact that all the policeman had vanished.

The Duma session was cut short, but after some vacillation the Duma leaders decided to remain informally in session. On 27 February a Provisional Committee was elected consisting of the leaders of the Progressive Bloc of the Duma plus some left-wing representatives—Alexander Kerensky, a temperamental young lawyer of Populist sympathies, and Nicholas Chkheidze, a Menshevik. This committee had nothing subversive in mind: it was simply supposed to "restore order and deal with institutions and individuals."

On the very same day, 27 February, in the Tauride Palace, the seat of the Duma, there convened, with no guidance, no mandate, and no plan, the Petrograd Soviet of Workers' Deputies, which on 2 March changed its name to the Soviet of Workers' and Soldiers' Deputies.

During the afternoon, while the Petrograd garrison was *de facto* sapping the foundations of the old regime, some left-wing Duma members, recently released political prisoners, and a variety of journalists, doctors, lawyers, Rural Council employees, and so on, had set up the Provisional Executive Committee of the Petrograd Soviet, which was not yet in existence, and in the evening hundreds of people of unknown antecedents held a plenary session of the Soviet confirming the Executive Committee.

The idea of reviving the 1905 revolutionary assembly seems to have sprung up by itself. No one has ever claimed credit for it; it must have occurred more or less simultaneously to a number of labor leaders and intellectuals. It should of course be emphasized that the Soviet—simply the Russian

At 10:00 in the morning of February 27, 1917 the subaltern Astakhov induced some soldiers of the Volhynia guard to leave their barracks. Without difficulty these persuaded their friends in other regiments to follow them, and soon all the soldiers of the Petrograd garrison were in the streets, mingling with the workers and singing the "Marseillaise." This is a typical scene from the first days of revolution.

word for *council,* a word retained by the Soviet Union—at that time did not have its present political connotation. In origin the Soviet was genuinely representative to some extent.

By 3 March the Soviet had 1,300 members, and a week later 3,000, of which 800 represented factory workers and the remainder various army units, a fact that is in itself significant since there were far more workers in Petrograd than soldiers.

Thus, even before the collapse of the Tsarist regime, the Tauride Palace became the seat of two sources of power that were more authoritative than the former government apparatus.

Thousands of soldiers and civilians began streaming into the vast and stately halls of the Palace; the whole building was turned into an arena for a shabby, headstrong, seething mass, with the more sedate quarters reserved for the Duma and its hangers-on.

By 2 March the Tsar had signed a document of abdication; the following day he was sent off by train with his family to captivity and ultimately death.

In the space of three days the apparently unshakable Tsarist administration had simply been short-circuited. Nothing was left of it—and this was felt by everyone in the capital.

The throngs of people teeming in and around the Tauride Palace had no clear objective. It was the conservative Fourth Duma that was first turned to by many of the upper- and middle-class Russians, who gravitated toward it as the new state authority.

The Soviet, a mass-meeting in many ways, was against the retention of the monarchy with or without Nicholas II. On 2 March, by the time a provisional government had been formed by the Provisional Committee of the Duma after a laboriously arrived-at agreement with the Executive Committee of the Soviet, it was evident that a constitutional monarchy, which had been hoped for by the conservative Duma leaders headed by Miliukov, was no longer a possibility. The insistence of the Soviet had excluded it, and the liberals, who had been hoping for the accession to the throne of the Tsar's brother, who would serve as regent for the Tsar's young son and heir Michael, were confronted by the *de facto* elimination of monarchism as a principle of government. The ancient Russian historical tradition was extinguished.

Despite the casualties of the upheaval—some 1,500—the monarchy had evaporated with fabulous ease. It had been short-circuited through the spontaneous behavior of the inhabitants of Petrograd, plus the disaffected garrison, and in the absence of any leadership. The rest of the country and the army as such played no role. The overturn of the government was accepted throughout the country, with or without enthusiasm, as an accomplished fact.

For eight months the destinies of Russia were to be played out in an arena of democratic expression against the background of the continuing war. Russia was freer than at any time in its history.

The Soviet leaders, almost uniformly Social-Revolutionaries and Mensheviks, did not contest the authority vested in the Provisional Government that had sprung out of the Fourth Duma. Their own authority had been forced on them long before the authority itself was juridically recognized, which did not actually take place until the eve of the Bolshevik insurrection in October. The trade unions, the industrial working class generally, and the peasants supported the Soviet. The trains would not move, the municipal institutions and the police were paralyzed, and the most basic functions of administration were inhibited unless authorized, sanctioned, or specifically ordered by the Soviet, which according to the official theory of the Provisional Government remained a private body. And despite the theoretical sovereignty of the Provisional Government, its authority was viable only through the grace of the Soviet, which declined to acknowledge its own authority in theory while in fact retaining control of all administration.

The Marxists in the Soviet—Mensheviks and Bolsheviks (the latter being represented before Lenin's arrival in April by Stalin and a young man, Vyacheslav Molotov)—could not take power; their political analysis prevented them. For Marxists, socialism could come about only after capitalism had matured, at which time the proletariat would also have matured sufficiently to be able to establish socialism. It seemed obvious that socialism was bound to fail in a backward, agrarian, semi-feudal country such as Russia.

During the eight months of the Provisional Government, accordingly, the Mensheviks, together with the Social-Revolutionaries, would do nothing to hamper the provisional government representing the bourgeoisie; the Marxists would at most act as the government's supervisors.

Lenin's arrival in April transformed this configuration; I shall merely situate him socially.

Vladimir Ilyich Ulyanov (Lenin) (1870–1924) was born into a prosperous family. His father was a professor of mathematics and an academic supervisor who had been given a noble title in accordance with the Table of Ranks. Lenin's mother was the daughter of a well-known physician. Educated by family tutors and governesses, she spoke four languages, sang, and played the piano. In short, Lenin belonged by birth to the landowning class.

Until he was twenty-seven the question of his earning a living never arose. Afterwards the combination of family and Party allowances, as well as what he made by his pen, enabled him to live in circumstances that were, materially speaking, perfectly bourgeois, though the personal frugality of Lenin and his wife, Nadezhda Krupskaya, made them indifferent to such questions.

On his return to Russia at the age of forty-seven, Lenin was merely the leader of a small group in the mini-universe of the Russian revolutionaries. No one could have foreseen that in a few months he was to become one of the most influential people in history.

In February 1917, when the food riots broke out, Lenin, together with many other revolutionaries, including Martov, was in Switzerland. The idea was conceived (apparently by Martov) of getting back to Russia via Germany. The German government was approached; it assented and provided the revolutionaries with a sealed train.

On his arrival Lenin made a switch in Marxist theory to the effect that a Marxist party could take power, after all, *legitimately*. The word is important—Marxist parties must buttress their behavior by theory. Lenin's theoretical switch immediately made him formidable politically.

The switch itself was based on an analysis generally attributed to Leon Trotsky, though Lenin had, as it seems, come to the same conclusion independently.

Leon Trotsky (1879–1940) was known as a brilliant speaker and a many-sided writer. Since becoming a celebrity amongst the Russian exiles after his precocious role as chairman of the short-lived Soviet of 1905, he had become a more or less full-time journalist with a revolutionary hobby. As a revolutionary he had had a position of his own outside the Bolshevik and Menshevik camps, which he made some futile efforts to reconcile. In effect Trotsky remained a maverick throughout the decade preceding 1917; he was distinguished, moreover, for the implacability of his attacks on Lenin, which he set forth in the usual guise of theoretical differences.

Trotsky's theory—patented, so to speak, as "permanent revolution"—held that the Russian bourgeoisie was too weak to overcome Tsarism alone and reform capitalism adequately before the Russian workers grew strong enough to push it out altogether; hence it was necessary for the working class to take power in order to accomplish the bourgeois revolution on behalf of the bourgeoisie, thus creating a situation in which the proletariat could construct socialism later on.

Lenin took up this theory in April; to the consternation of his comrades, he insisted that the Bolsheviks must take power and waste no more time waiting for the Russian bourgeoisie to reform capitalism.

Lenin arrived in the evening of 3 April at the Finland Station of Petrograd. Though unknown at this time outside political circles, he was welcomed by a huge throng that filled the square. His speech ended with a slogan that at the time was utterly alien to all socialists in Russia, including the Bolsheviks—"Long live the socialist revolution."

Sukhanov, a semi-Menshevik journalist and economist who has left us the only full-length memoir of the turbulent eight months of 1917, slipped into the celebration of Lenin's arrival in the Bolshevik headquarters, where he had been driven from the Finland Station on top of an armored car, "holding a service," as Sukhanov says, at every street crossing to gaping crowds.

Sukhanov gives us a vivid description not only of Lenin's oratorical style, but of the emotional impact of his break with socialist tradition. Even though Lenin, while not yet ikonized, had immense authority within his faction, his new theory flabbergasted his disciples—he had to conquer them before aquiring a mass following. Here is Sukhanov's eye-witness account:

> The celebrated master of the order got to his feet. I shall never forget that thunderlike speech, which startled and amazed not only me, a heretic who had accidentally dropped in, but all the true believers. I am certain that no one had expected anything of the sort. It seemed as though all the elements had risen from their abodes, and the spirit of universal destruction, knowing neither barriers nor doubts, neither human difficulties nor human calculations, were hovering around Kshesinskaya's reception room above the heads of the bewitched disciples.
>
> Lenin was a very good orator—not an orator of the consummate, rounded phrase, or of the luminous image, or of absorbing pathos or of the pointed witticism, but an orator of enormous impact and power, breaking down complicated systems into the simplest and most generally accessible elements, and hammering, hammering, hammering them into the heads of his audience until he took them captive.

Sukhanov goes on to give us some typical reflections of Lenin's opponents:

191

Skobelev told Miliukov about his (Lenin's) "lunatic ideas," appraising him as a completely lost man standing outside the movement. I agreed in general with this estimate of Lenin's ideas and said that in his present guise he was so unacceptable to everyone that now he was not at all dangerous for our interlocutor, Miliukov. However, the future of Lenin seemed different to me: I was convinced that after he had escaped from his foreign academic milieu and entered an atmosphere of real struggle and wide practical activity, he would acclimatise himself quickly, settle down, stand on firm ground, and throw overboard the bulk of his anarchist "ravings." What life failed to accomplish with him, the solid pressure of his party comrades would help with. I was convinced that in the near future Lenin would again be converted into a herald of the ideas of revolutionary Marxism and occupy a place in the revolution worthy of him as the most authoritative leader of the Soviet proletarian left. Then, I said, he would be dangerous to Miliukov. And Miliukov agreed with me.

We refused to admit that Lenin might stick to his "abstractions." Still less did we admit that through these abstractions Lenin would be able to conquer not only the revolution, not only all its active masses, not only the whole Soviet—but even his own Bolsheviks.

We were cruelly mistaken. . . .

During the eight months of the Provisional Government, all parties, except for the Bolsheviks after Lenin's arrival, supported the war. This burden, inherited from Tsarism, was to undo the Provisional Government and pave the way to the Bolshevik putsch. The war situation was or seemed to be hopeless: the material difficulties kept accumulating, and though there was a certain amount of enthusiasm at times for the Provisional Government, and though Kerensky often seemed genuinely popular, the hardships of war, plus its unpopularity, made the task of the middle-class government, as well as of the Social-Revolutionaries and the Mensheviks who supported it, in practical terms impossible.

There was another factor, in any case, that was to prove crucial. It may be called the secret background of the Bolshevik putsch—unsuspected at the time even by knowledgeable insiders like Sukhanov (though his silence—under the Bolsheviks—may have been tactful).

Lenin did in fact have an organic relationship with the German government—though not an agent, he was undoubtedly an ally. Since he was the only Russian revolutionary demanding an end to the war—for the Germans, i.e., the immobilization of the eastern front—he played a vital role. Beginning no later than the spring of 1917, the German government had put a very large sum of money at the disposal of the Bolsheviks.

It was more than 60 million gold marks, or, in today's currency about $1,000 million. This sum, staggering by any reckoning, though of course a bagatelle for a regime sustaining millions of soldiers on two fronts, enabled the Bolsheviks to maintain a vast press (forty-one periodicals) that hammered away at public opinion with the simplest of slogans— none of them Marxist in the slightest—and thus made the Bolsheviks both respectable and popular. This ramified press was undoubtedly a factor in the Bolshevik triumph in October.

The subsidies also played a considerable role in Bolshevik politics.

One of the first acts of the Provisional Government was to proclaim the liberty of the press. Seen here are the new revolutionary newspapers being distributed to the crowd. The main Marxist papers were Izvestia *(The News), organ of the Executive Committee of the Soviet,* Novaya Zhizn *(New Life) of Gorky and* Pravda *(Truth), publication of the Bolsheviks, which was Lenin's platform (he took the title from Trotsky).*

Trotsky had worked out "Permanent Revolution," his own twist on Marxist theory, together with another Russian Jewish Marxist some twelve years older than himself, Alexander Israel Helphand (1867–1923), who had made a name for himself as editor and writer in the German Social-Democratic movement and during the 1905 upset had collaborated with Trotsky, who had the highest opinion of his brainpower. Helphand had gone to the Balkans a few years before the outbreak of the 1914 war and made a fortune as a businessman: he was, no doubt, the first Marxist multimillionaire in history. It was he who had proposed to the German government that it subsidize the revolutionaries.

In July 1917, when in the midst of the unremitting turbulence the Bolsheviks were thought, perhaps rightly, to be preparing a putsch, the news of the German subsidy leaked out in the form of documents that were so puerile as to suggest that they might have been planted on the Kerensky government; Lenin and his top aides bolted immediately. Plainly, they could not afford a full-dress inquiry; it had to do, after all, with high treason in wartime.

Trotsky, not a Bolshevik at the time, was not subject to the same charge as Lenin; while Lenin was in hiding, Trotsky *became* a Bolshevik *in order* to make the putsch. Using his influence as Chairman of the Soviet, to which he was elected in the autumn of 1917, Trotsky stage-managed the putsch and, moreover, in the teeth of Lenin's objections, presented it as a Soviet enterprise. In the event, this rallied the bulk of left-wing and even liberal opinion to the new regime and enabled the Bolsheviks to survive the civil war after the putsch. Trotsky's remarkably successful imposture was to survive in the name of the Soviet Union.

Lenin and Trotsky had concurred in a Marxist justification of a socialist party's taking power, even in a backward agrarian country, as a way of imposing a bourgeois revolution on the bourgeoisie. But this required a further justification—it was assumed that once the socialist party was in power in such a country, the revolution that was thought to be imminent in the advanced industrial countries would come to the rescue of such a socialist outpost.

Lenin and Trotsky were convinced that the big revolution was bound to break out, at the very least in Germany, the industrial heart of Europe. By October 1917 Lenin was transported; it seemed to him that Germany was on the point of exploding. On 7 October he wrote that "the worldwide workers' revolution had begun . . . doubts are impossible. We stand on the threshold of the world proletarian revolution."

It was against the background of this general expectation that the decision was taken at a secret meeting of the Central Committee, on 10 October, with twelve of the twenty-one members present. The discussion (which took place, curiously enough, in Sukhanov's flat, without his knowledge) lasted for about ten hours. Lenin's resolution that the "armed insurrection is inevitable and the time for it fully ripe" was passed by ten to two (Lenin's two intimates, Zinoviev and Kamenev, voted against it).

The Bolshevik putsch proved to be child's play. As Lenin said later, "it was as easy as lifting up a feather." With the Marxist justification of the putsch reserved for the Party elite, the masses were appealed to by the enormous, German-subsidized press on the basis of a broad campaign summed up in three words—peace, bread, land.

In Lenin's absence Trotsky, Chairman of the Soviet since 23 September and moreover Chairman of the Military Revolutionary Committee set up by the Soviet for the "revolutionary defense" of Petrograd, created the strategy of the putsch. The idea was simple, the putsch was led up to through preparations that were presented as a general defense of the Soviet. Though the plan itself—as Trotsky was to admit—was crude, hasty and improvised, and for that matter publicly discussed before-hand, it was enough: the Bolsheviks' opponents were strangely indolent.

On the night of 24 October the Military Revolutionary Committee sent armed detachments to occupy the key points of the capital's railway terminals, bridges, state banks, telephone exchange, central post office, and various public buildings. Though the troops were apathetic, they were at any rate not against the Bolsheviks, except for a few neutral regiments, including the Cossacks; there was no bloodshed or opposition. The next day nearly all the ministers of the Provisional Government were arrested, except for Kerensky, who escaped abroad. They were taken to the Peter-Paul Fortress to join their Tsarist predecessors.

The putsch was so easy that no one was aware of what was happening. Most of the shops, theaters, and cinemas were open: on the afternoon of 25 October, when the putsch was supposedly at its height, city life looked practically normal.

That same afternoon Trotsky took time off to preside over a session of the Petrograd Soviet. Lenin, who had been in hiding from the Provisional Government since July, finally emerged to take over publicly the reins of power seized by his Party. After the preceding months of tension, wrangling, and apathy, the mood was now very enthusiastic. Sukhanov reports the scene:

Long-drawn-out ovations alternated with the singing of "The Internationale." Lenin was hailed again, hurrahs were shouted, caps flung into the air. A funeral march was sung in memory of the martyrs of the war. Then they applauded again, shouted, flung up their caps. The whole Presidium, headed by Lenin, was standing up and singing, with exalted faces and blazing eyes. . . . Applause, hurrahs, caps flung up into the air. . . .

Lenin's entourage had undertaken a momentous gamble. A tiny minority, with no control of the population and with no administrative personnel, had embarked on the government of a large, backward, agrarian country. Shortly after the putsch, moreover, the Bolsheviks had dispersed the Constituent assembly—the dream of generations of Russian revolutionaries, including the Bolsheviks themselves before the putsch. Thus the handful of Bolshevik leaders were to exercise a monopoly.

They had, in fact, replaced the working out of economic forces as analyzed by classical Marxism with political decisions, improvised *ad hoc.* What is more, they took this road alone. The failure of the revolution to sweep Europe—there were a few fiascoes after the war in Germany and Hungary—isolated the Bolsheviks.

A striking instance of Bolshevik improvisation was their promise of land to the peasants. A land decree abolished all private ownership in land, making it impossible to buy, sell, lease, mortgage, or alienate land in any way. This scheme, which revived the most unworkable features of the antiquated village commune, was lifted bodily from the arsenal of Social-Revolutionary theory, which the Bolsheviks had been laughing at for years. Lenin defended this incorporation of his opponents' theories as—expedient.

The Bolsheviks had not, of course, worked out a plan to remake society. In Lenin's words, "The point is the seizure of power; afterwards we shall see what we can do with it."

Thus the Bolsheviks, intellectually rooted in Marxist abstractions and without practical plans, were determined to maintain their monopoly by reshaping society. The large-scale goals to be lumped together as "Socialism" (now distinct from "Communism," far in the future) amounted to the control by the State—i.e., the Party—of all social and economic activities.

CHAPTER X

THE NEO-BOLSHEVIK STATE

The legacy of the war was disastrous. Russia lay prostrate. Even if the Bolsheviks in making their putsch had had a concrete scheme of social reconstruction, they would have been incapable of implementing it. Their energies were consumed by ending the war with the Germans and defending themselves against the "White" opposition in the civil war and various foreign forces (Great Britain, the United States). The combination of civil war and foreign intervention went on for more than four years.

The Bolsheviks were a unique phenomenon in world history: enthralled by faith in a complex of ideas—the Marxist system—they transformed the society under their control independently of the real-life concerns of ordinary people. The ultimate goal of the Bolsheviks was to transform a living society into an entirely different society—an ideal society.

But once the Bolsheviks seized power in a backward peasant country, and set about installing socialism by force, it was no longer possible to look to Marxism for guidance. Marx had regarded all writers of blueprints for the future as mere idiots; his sole concern had been the road leading to the assumption of power by the proletariat.

Instead, the Bolsheviks, claiming to represent the proletariat, had taken power with the aim of totally transforming a backward society via an administration that encompassed all aspects of life. The titanic dimensions of such a project brought about the gargantuan magnification of its administration.

Thus the Bolsheviks had put themselves beyond Marxism practically by the very fact of their putsch: the tiny Bolshevik nucleus was obviously not the proletariat, nor was it possible to explain from a Marxist point of view their seizure of power.

This contradictory situation gave rise to the outstanding phenomenon in the politics of the twentieth century: the consolidation of Marxism as a state cult at the very moment that its fundamental ideas were contradicted. Marxism had proved to be irrelevant to the evolution of capitalism; all its predictions had misfired. It had ignored the two outstanding phenomena of the modern age—technology and the rise of a vast middle class. Marxism was also irrelevant to the problems of Russia under Bolshevism, but the Bolsheviks in power could enforce their own view of Marxism, despite its manifest irrelevance, as the framework of all society and indeed of all life.

The Bolsheviks accommodated these ideological difficulties in their own way by instantly creating the concept of "Leninism." Yet the true meaning of "Marxist-Leninist" is concealed by the obvious prominence of Lenin. It really implies something quite different, i.e., that the putsch led by Lenin *contradicted* Marxism, though this could not be said, so to speak, in public: it referred to the role played by individual action, and also to the clandestine activities of the new regime in defending itself against the world by an overwhelming concentration on networks of espionage. Thus each half of "Marxist-Lenist" had an implied significance.

It was the need of laying down a line to which obedience could be compelled that transformed Marxism, now Marxism-Leninism, into a state cult in which only one interpretation was authoritative. For who, after all, could distinguish between possible interpretations of Marxist abstractions? In the Soviet Union this was almost immediately to be only the faction with the power to do so. This monolithic, quasi-ecclesiastical structure was to dominate the Soviet Union from 1917 on.

The Bolsheviks began with a regime of "war communism," which merely meant the expropriation of all major institutions: the banks, the merchant marine, the grain dealers, the mines, and the oil industry, as well as all enterprises with a capital of between a half-million and a million rubles. Only business with fewer than ten workers were left untouched. This first attempt at centralized direction was done so amateurishly, against such a background of devastation, that when the civil war was over, the country was substantially reduced.

Vast areas had been lying fallow for years. The battlefields had been shifting constantly, especially in the Ukraine, where the destruction was general; harvests had been destroyed over and over again. Industry was completely shattered: production was down to a seventh of the prewar figure. Most of the factories were standing idle: many mines had been physically annihilated. Pig-iron production amounted to only 3 percent of what it had been before the war. The stocks of metal and industrial products were exhausted; food and fuel were unavailable. The workers were discontented: wages had been lost by the shutting-down of factories for lack of raw materials and fuel.

Commerce also had been halted. Small as well as large businesses were shut down; private trading was altogether prohibited in 1920. All cash had to be deposited in the state bank, all precious metals surrendered.

The early enthusiasm that had attended the Bolshevik putsch and the excitement of the civil war had evaporated. The Bolsheviks found themselves holding an utterly ruined country that in addition had lost practically all its educated classes. After the Bolshevik putsch some 3–4 million Russians, nearly all of them belonging to the aristocracy and cultivated classes, emigrated, leaving the Bolsheviks the immensely difficult problem of finding and training technicians and administrators.

This historically unique exodus had been brought about with no propaganda: a few instances of thugs shooting people with "white hands," in trains, were enough. Word spread like lightning.

The new role of the state made all economic activities political *ipso facto*. Having replaced the private employer, the state now collected all revenue from production: thus it played the same supervisory role as the private employer before it, with of course, the added advantage of a potent police force. Thus the Bolshevik slogan, "socialization of the means of production," meant in practice a highly centralized network of production subordinate to the governing apparatus and backed by a concentrated police power. This was duplicated, on the consumers' side, by the vast bureaucracy required for large-scale distribution.

The Bolsheviks found themselves outflanked on the left; to defend themselves they ruthlessly smashed the Kronstadt uprising. The Kronstadt garrison—14,000 men, 10,000 of them sailors—was wiped out by March. The survivors of the Bolshevik attack, which encountered ferocious resistance, were shot or sent to prison camps.

The Kronstadt insurrection was the first of the feuds within the Bolshevik fold. With its dense intermixture of political and economic factors, the insurrection was an obvious danger-symptom; it was clear that a way out of the economic quagmire had to be found. The conclusions Lenin first drew from the Kronstadt mutiny involved a tightening of the security police system to forestall the danger of any further mutinies, but ultimately the mutiny made him turn aside from the program of planning—a national planning commission had been established in the early part of February 1921—and look for a radically different way out of the devastation exacerbated by the chaos of war communism.

The Bolshevik solution was a return to capitalism: the regime, still too weak to plan on a national scale, had to stimulate the peasants' interest in producing for a market. It had to ensure the food supply, start up commerce again, and fortify the industrial plant.

The Bolsheviks, while tightening the controls essential for their monopoly, made a bold about-face. In the New Economic Policy (March 1921) they established a mixed economy; the concerns that still remained nationalized were to compete with reborn private enterprise. The theory was that the socialized sector of the economy would gradually grow at the expense of the private sector, but that this would come about through the natural operation of economic forces, not by political action. The large industrial plants, transport, the banking system, and foreign trade were to remain the monopoly of the state; the rest of the industrial sector and domestic trade were to be open to private initiative. The right to private ownership was restored within limits; the peasants could again sell some of their produce on the open market. Foreign capital was solicited, and foreign firms were invited back to Russia, even into heavy industry. This Bolshevik surrender to capitalism went hand in hand with generally successful attempts, via treaties and trade pacts to restore international relations with the non-Bolshevik world.

The country gradually recovered: production started up again, in both agriculture and industry, and commerce became much livelier in the money economy restored by the N.E.P. By the beginning of 1923 the economy began to look viable for the first time in seven years.

Academic and university education, severely curtailed during the civil war, began to revive. Education met with the greatest difficulties; Russia's intellectual life had almost collapsed during the years of crisis. Vast numbers of intellectuals, who belonged chiefly to the upper classes, had died in prisons or been killed by hunger and cold. The chief scholars of Russia had joined the huge White emigration. But during the N.E.P., education revived substantially, initially with the collaboration of the bourgeois experts who had managed to survive.

Moreover, there was a great efflorescence of artistic creativity during the first decade of Bolshevik rule. Some original poets became prominent—Yesenin, Mayakovsky, Blok, and Pasternak. In music Prokofiev and Stravinsky were very influential; Shostakovich was perhaps the best known of the younger composers. An immense international impression also was made by the cinema; Eisenstein's films were considered a stunning innovation. The theater and ballet revived once again, to be sure without any novelties. In the arts the tendencies that had been considered decadent were now hailed as expressions of the vanguard.

Even the Bolshevik excesses during the first decade after the putsch exemplified, in the purely social sphere, a utopian enthusiasm. The feeling of fruitful break-up felt by many socialists throughout Europe, for instance, at the prospect of the first socialist party in history actually taking power, reflected itself in a general euphoria among intellectuals.

The ancient tradition of the family came under attack as a bourgeois institution; marriage and sexual morality were much chuckled over; sexual license, concomitantly, was lauded. Discipline in schools was castigated as the height of reactionary outrageousness. Religion—according to Marx the "opiate of the people"—was of course anathema to all official circles, though the churches, while deprived of funds and generally speaking squeezed and propagandized against, were not actually proscribed.

This relatively liberal situation lasted until about 1928— the watershed in the evolution of the Bolshevik monopoly.

Though the new regime was to "justify" everything it did by references to Marxism, in fact Marxism had nothing to tell them: all Marxist analysis, and prediction stopped with the seizure of power by the Proletariat whose representatives the Bolsheviks proclaimed themselves to be.

Divergent views were expressed within the summits of the Party even before Lenin's death in January 1924. But decisions were reached not by a process of debate but as a result of organizational politics—the administrative apparatus, in full control of Russia, became the focus of Bolshevik authority.

The apparatus had, inevitably, appeared overnight. As the Bolshevik Party, originally a coterie of agitators, conspirators, speakers, and writers, began coping with practical matters, it was transformed into a corps of administrators. And to the extent that Bolshevik controls blanketed the whole country and all aspects of life, both social and economic, the role of the administrators was bound to be all the more comprehensive.

Anyone controlling the Party obviously controlled the country, and as the prospects of the revolution faded, leaving the Bolsheviks isolated in a very large country, the specific weight of the apparatus grew by leaps and bounds. Concomitantly, the power of the General Secretary—in charge of all personnel appointments, the allocation of functions, and of government procedure—expanded.

Joseph Stalin had been appointed General Secretary in 1921, while Lenin was still in full vigor. It was Stalin, accordingly, who was to formulate all Party decisions.

The idea that socialism could be confined to one country, however large, would hitherto have been nonsensical to any Marxist. Socialism, as the next higher stage of social organization after capitalism, naturally had to cover at least a substantial section of the world economy, and in any case had to have an advanced industrial base of its own to operate on.

This had been a Bolshevik commonplace up to 1924. In the early part of 1924, for instance, in his *Foundations of Leninism*, Stalin agreed that the proletariat might seize power in a single country, but could never create a socialist economy. No single country, however large, was enough to ensure socialism.

During two and a half years of civil war, Trotsky travelled along the fronts held by the sixteen armies which he galvanized and directed. He led the military operations against the Whites, and organized propaganda for the civilian population.

Lenin haranguing the crowd in 1919, while Trotsky listens at the foot of the platform. The two Bolshevik chiefs had complementary gifts: Trotsky's imagination and dynamism were constructively counterbalanced by Lenin's more considered personality.

In the records left by the Soviet government and by its internal critics—notably Trotsky—the middle twenties were dominated by a "struggle for power" between Stalin's central faction and Trotsky. Yet a glance at the actual succession of events will make it clear that there was no struggle whatever. As Stalin consolidated his government through his office of General Secretary, he merely used the influence that was naturally his in order to give all decisions the appearance of institutional support. Since Marxist jargon was the natural idiom of the Party, and since it took a few years before the Bolsheviks outside Stalin's entourage were reduced to silence, it was natural for all activity to be expressed in the conventional idiom. Since this suited both Stalin, for obvious reasons, and his opponents, principally Trotsky, for reasons still more obvious, it has been easy for historians, poring over the records, to accept the official version.

The draft program proclaimed by Stalin in 1927 was ratified by the Fifteenth Party Congress in December. Stalin set two cardinal goals for the Soviet economy—the massive civilization of agriculture and the intensified industrialization of the country.

It was the first attempt in history to encompass the entire economy of a nation under one centralized agency in one unified plan that even took in the boundless ramifications of retail distribution.

A State Planning Commission was entrusted with the elaboration of the first Five-Year Plan. The collectivization program was initiated in 1928. Involving a vast overturn in agricultural relations, it had a political side: before the program could be implemented, the "rich" peasants—*kulaks*—

had to be eliminated. The collectivization drive was launched, in fact, on the official theory that the rich peasants had to be curbed. An "offensive against the *kulaks*" was the slogan of the big drive.

But the collectivization movement built up its own momentum so quickly that private agriculture was soon explicitly proscribed. By the end of 1929 Stalin called for the "liquidation of the *kulaks* as a class"; in 1929 the *kulaks* were wiped out—or rather, to put it more accurately, all those who were wiped out were called *kulaks*.

The peasants were determined not to turn over to the government what they regarded as theirs: vast quantities of food were stored away, the cattle scheduled for the new farms were slaughtered, the crops were burned, the tools were smashed. The peasants calculated that such tactics would halt the government's crash program and force it back into a reasonable attitude.

They were sadly mistaken. Since mere administrative measures were futile, the government turned the army loose as well as the political police. Mutinous villages were surrounded by units with machine-guns and forced to surrender. The *kulaks*, both real *kulaks* and those suddenly called *kulaks* because of their opposition to collectivization, were rounded up in droves and deported to Arctic regions by the hundreds of thousands. By the end of 1929, as Stalin said, even expropriation was no longer sufficient: the *kulaks* had to be excluded from the collective farms entirely. Millions of peasants of all kinds were exiled, jailed, or killed.

This violence had been so unexpected that by March 1930 Stalin was forced to modulate the crash program. He did this, characteristically, by blaming the functionaries, who had become "dizzy with success." Thus Stalin gave a modern counterpoint to a traditional theme—bureaucrats were responsible for thwarting the benevolent Tsar!

This catastrophe created an unprecedented famine. In spite of official silence, the news leaked out; the regime was forced to admit that literally millions of people died of hunger in the governmentally induced famine of the early thirties. At Yalta, after the Second World War, Stalin told Winston Churchill that 10 million peasants had been eliminated. He did not mention the vast numbers—hundreds of thousands, according to Bukharin—including women and children, who were machine-gunned by special political police detachments.

The successive Five-Year Plans were to become the foundations of the Soviet Union. The vast Russian sacrifices in consumption created a large-scale technical elite and an immense concentration on heavy industry. Stalin was undoubtedly the consolidator, if not the founder, of Soviet power.

In consonance with the concentration of power within the Bolshevik apparatus, the political scene, too, became increasingly monolithic. After a short period of indulgence, the Bolsheviks, having dispersed the Constituent Assembly, began cracking down on all political expression.

A general campaign soon followed, first against the Mensheviks, then against the Social-Revolutionaries; by February 1922 arrests—the first of a long, long series—began to be made against the Bolsheviks' former fellow-revolutionaries. In the summer of 1922 the first political "trial" mounted by the Bolshevik Party took place; it was aimed at the Social-Revolutionaries. The court handed down fourteen death sentences and only two acquittals. The Social-Revolutionary movement, heir of so much agrarian, communizing, and anarchist tradition, was annihilated.

The suppression of all Left-wing, non-Bolshevik currents was followed very quickly by the beginnings of repression against dissident opinion within the Bolshevik Party. The repression of the Workers' Opposition, then the banning of the Left Opposition, in December 1927 (Trotsky, Zinoviev, Kamenev), culminated in the suppression of the Right Opposition (Bukharin) shortly after the onslaught on the *kulaks* early in 1928.

With the intensification of the crash campaign of collectivization, in fact, the Right Opposition, whose polemics had been used by Stalin in order to manipulate Party opinion against the Left Opposition, was itself distanced from the Stalin "center." The Right Opposition found itself in exactly the same position as the Left Opposition before, this time without even a Left Opposition to counterbalance Stalin's now overwhelming power. By pulverizing both Oppositions in turn, Stalin was now in unquestioned control of the entire Soviet government.

State power gave a new dimension to Bolshevik policy. For with Stalin's ousting of all opponents within the Party, a new institution was created—the secular cult of Soviet orthodoxy.

In full view of his own generation Stalin was glorified beyond all imagining. In the nine years between Lenin's fiftieth birthday in 1920—a very modest affair—and Stalin's in December 1929, the Soviet government, within the Bolshevik strait jacket, had expanded immeasurably. At the very pinnacle of the structure, Stalin, whirled aloft by the process he was instrumental in promoting, became a quasideity—the Godhead of the Soviet Trinity of Party, State, and Doctrine.

A 1920 poster showing Lenin delivering a speech from a lofty construction under a sign in Russian bearing the word "proletariat." The artist, El Lissitsky, had been in the vanguard of the modern movement in the early Soviet period. He remained in favor by switching to far more conventional forms of applied art.

The Grey House by Marc Chagall, 1917. Paul Pechère coll. Brussels. All his life Chagall has continued to paint poetic evocations of his native Russian town, Vitebsk, as it was in the first decades of the century. He had left the family isba and the farm animals that appear in so many of his canvases for Paris, in 1910. At the outbreak of the war he returned to Russia, and after the revolution he was put in charge of Fine Arts in his region. Like other artists such as Kandinsky, Pevsner and Gabo who also became émigrés, Chagall had expected to continue his work unhampered. But soon the rigidity of Stalinist rule stamped out all individual expression and Chagall left his country for good. He has lived in France since then.

During the Stalin era, from Stalin's fiftieth birthday in 1929 to his death in 1953, he was invariably referred to in language hitherto reserved for semidivine personages such as Muhammad and the Buddha, though not, to be sure, Jesus Christ.

Framed by the new cult, the Bolshevik state, having weathered the crash campaigns of collectivization and industrialization, might have seemed firmly embedded in the nation. The cult of Stalin the Genius, Locomotive of the World Revolution and Father of the Peoples, had finally stabilized Soviet life, as it seemed, and socialist construction, whatever its content, now constituted the balanced framework of a zealous society busily reworking its destinies.

Yet Bolshevik totalitarianism was not yet rounded off. Despite appearances—despite the censorship, despite the monolithic state, despite the repression—the consummation of the Stalin regime had yet to be achieved. The peoples of the Soviet Union were to be put through another threshing machine.

In December 1934 Sergei Kirov, Secretary of the Party in Leningrad, was assassinated. His assassin was said to be a former Young Communist. The assassination triggered a series of arrests, hearings, and executions that culminated in the "Moscow Show Trials" of 1936–38—a unique phenomenon.

There were three such Show Trials, in 1936, 1937, and 1938; differing in some trivial details, they were all frantically publicized and marked the elimination of all the "Old Bolsheviks."

Zinoviev, Kamenev, Radek, Bukharin, and many others were accused of being agents of Leon Trotsky—in exile at the time—in a conspiracy he had entered into with Hitler, the Mikado of

Japan, and the British Secret Service to murder the Politburo, dismember the Soviet Union, and restore capitalism.

The Show Trials were characterized, in particular, by the well-nigh complete absence of any evidence and by the confessions of the prisoners vilifying themselves in an hysteria that kept pace with the denunciations of the prosecutor. With a couple of exceptions, all the Old Bolsheviks were executed immediately after their "trial."

The Show Trials, while giving rise to occasional doubts outside the Soviet Union, were accepted fairly unanimously by the world press. Trotsky defended himself as best he could, together with his son Sedov—his "accomplice" in Paris—but despite exhausting efforts he could not counteract the impression made by the Trials.

A few years after Stalin's death, Nikita Khrushchev, one of his successors, in a famous secret speech to the Twentieth Party Congress in 1956, made it clear that the Moscow Show Trials were, quite simply, fabrications.

Khrushchev's secret speech confirmed what in any case had been established by a large literature that had begun appearing in the fifties. This literature, though somewhat fragmented—memoirs of deserters, defectors, and survivors— sketched in the outlines of a remarkable enterprise, nothing less than a broad-gauge scheme for the reordering of Soviet society. Stalin, personally responsible for Kirov's assassination, exploited it for his large-scale projects.

The Show Trials, in fact, were in no sense of the word trials, not even in the sense of being frame-ups. They were actually propaganda cast in the form of charades, contrived by Stalin to achieve certain psychopolitical objectives.

217

The Great Charades cast as Show Trials served as an umbrella for a process of far broader scope that was carried on relatively secretly, was never admitted to by the Soviet leadership, and has never, in fact, been acknowledged. Outside the Soviet Union this process was known later on as the Great Purge, though here again the word purge was itself an aspect of Stalin's propaganda. It was not remotely a purge of the Party such as the Soviet public had grown familiar with during the expansion of constraints beginning with the early twenties: it was, rather, a Deep Comb-out of the population as a whole, in which millions of citizens, also accused of complicity with Trotsky in his conspiracy with Hitler to restore capitalism, were put through a wringer.

The tidal wave of arrests in the Deep Comb-out that began with the Great Charades of 1936–38 engulfed all former oppositionists of all kinds, former Mensheviks and S.R.s, anarchists, members of the Jewish Bund, Zionists, sympathizers of prerevolutionary Left-wing parties, returned immigrants, Party people whose duties had sent them abroad, everyone who had corresponded with anyone abroad, foreign communists taking refuge in the Soviet Union, members of all religious sects, anyone who had ever been excluded from the Party, any Party member who had resisted the purging process itself, and representatives of all ethnic minorities. All strata of the population were represented, from top to bottom, and all occupations.

Most striking was the decapitation of the government apparatus itself; of the 140 members of the Central Committee in 1934, for instance, only 15 were still free in 1937.

Perhaps the most spectacular aspect of the Deep Comb-out was its catastrophic effect on the armed forces. With Europe dominated by Nazi Germany, Stalin raked out the Red Army. During 1937–38 he cut down the membership of the Supreme War Council by 75 percent, killed 3 out of 5 marshals, 13 out of 15 army generals, 62 out of 85 corps commanders, 110 out of 195 divisional commanders, and 220 out of 406 brigade commanders. Probably 65 percent of the officers from colonel up were arrested, numbering, together with those in the lower echelons arrested, some 20,000 officers. Of the 6,000 high-ranking officers, 1,500 were killed; others vanished into various forms of detention.

The slaughter of 1936–38 is conservatively assessed as having destroyed between 5 and 10 percent of the population—perhaps 8.5 million victims. Many think the figure was nearer 20 million.

In 1940 Trotsky was assassinated in Mexico by an agent of Stalin's a couple of years after his son Sedov's murder in Paris. Trotsky had spent four years in exile in Turkey after his deportation from the Soviet Union in 1929; after flitting about in France for a brief, uneasy period, he found refuge first in Norway and then, after being forced out of Norway by the Soviet government, in Mexico, where he continued his lone, practically unaided fight against the stupefying effects of the Great Charades.

The Great Charades and the Deep Comb-out are generally relegated to the dead past—a grotesque episode blurred by remoteness. Yet this brief period of extravagant bloodshed to the accompaniment of ghoulish elements of blanket betrayal surely consolidated the neo-Bolshevik state.

The practical elements in the Charades and Comb-out—their merely utilitarian benefits—were minor. They provided convenient scapegoats, to be sure, for the grueling hardships

219

and endless blunders of the Five-Year Plans, the crash collectivization campaign, the poor harvests, and the famines. Yet it
is plain that they served a far more profound purpose.

The Great Charades and Deep Comb-out consummated a
process, initiated in the twenties, that established the secular
cult of Soviet orthodoxy. They provided orthodoxy with the
counterpoint required, perhaps, by all orthodoxy—its polar
opposite.

The disagreements on policy that had beset the Party in the
early twenties were emotionalized in the space of a few years.
As it became necessary to replace the dogma of world revolution with the dogma of socialism in one country, the verbiage
generated by Marxist bickering took on a special theological
tinge. The Stalin apparatus, while pretending to take classical
Marxism as the basis of decisions, in reality enforced them
through the administrative machine.

There was a remarkably steep jump in the intensity of
the official reaction to Trotsky's views beginning in 1924.
Attacked at first as merely incorrect, Trotsky's ideas were
swiftly projected as the reflection of an inherent wronghead-
edness; by the mid-thirties they were equated with evil itself.

The theologizing tendency of the Bolshevik apparatus may
be seen in the new scriptures authorized by Stalin. The
writings of Marx, Engels, and of course Lenin were a natural
object of reverence; in 1938, the last year of the Bolshevik
massacre, the dialectical materialism underlying, in theory,
the Bolshevik state was crystallized in an official textbook—
*A Short Course in the History of the Communist Party of
the Soviet Union.* All Marxist writings outside this textbook, including the writings of Lenin himself, were in effect
proscribed.

Stalin had condensed all Marxism in the new textbook, the only authorized guide to the interpretation of the Marxist scriptures proper.

Essentially, the *Short Course* consummated the total rewriting of *all* history begun with Stalin's justification, in 1924, of the shift from Revolution to socialism in one country. In the thirties Stalin, obliged to explain how it was that all Old Bolsheviks except Lenin and Stalin had been maniacs and traitors, had to have the entire history of the Party rewritten from top to bottom, as well as all encyclopedias and reference works.

The *Short Course*, plus the satanization of Trotsky, consummated the Soviet cult of orthodoxy. The massacre of 5 to 10 percent of the population engraved that cult in the flesh of the people—if Marxism did not fit the Soviet people, then the people had to be reshaped in order to fit Soviet Marxism. The "proud flesh" of the population—all those who were superfluous, recalcitrant, or potentially so—was lopped off. Others were terrified.

Bolshevik mythology was thus created to justify the existence of the Bolshevik state. The concept underlying the Great Charades and their concomitant massacre—encirclement outside and betrayal inside—was given a theological foundation—the forces of light under Stalin and the true party were contending with the forces of darkness under Trotsky and the hosts of hell. Thus the satanization of Trotsky created a formula flexible enough to encompass all aspects of dissidence and nonconformism, genuine or alleged, within the framework of the all-inclusive concept of a non-existent "Trotskyism." This ingredient of Stalinism was to survive for decades, even in the agitation for the "reforms" of the 1980s.

The consummation of this theological process may very well have been accelerated by the menace that began looming up with the victory of the Nazi movement in January 1933, when Adolf Hitler was elected German Chancellor. Though at first sight it might seem irrational on Stalin's part to mutilate the Red Army at the very moment a powerful enemy was arming at breakneck pace, it seems plain that the very menace to the Soviet state made Stalin's decision to re-order its inner structure all the more urgent.

During the thirties, the Party itself changed radically as a new elite grew in tandem with the economy. The working class element in it, relatively exiguous even during the twenties, dwindled to less than a third, while the new intelligentsia—Party officials, the upper strata of academic life, executives, managers—came to about half. From the thirties on, the social origins of Party members were a well-kept secret.

The Eighteenth Party Congress (March 1929) erased even the fictitious pre-eminence of the working class; by promoting the intelligentsia, in the broadest sense, to equality with workers and peasants, the Congress established the social primacy of upper government functionaries. This itself was anchored in the status of the Party as a mass institution: still only 500,000 in 1923, five years after the putsch, it had become a mass organization by 1934 (3.5 million). During the mid-twenties, Stalin in his initial domestic skirmishes, had been diluting the Party with more or less illiterate recruits in order to swamp his opponents: in 1925–26 alone 200,000 new members were admitted. Then the Party was cut back; by the beginning of the Second World War it was somewhat more than 2.3 million. Since then it has been relatively on the increase, discounting the casualties of the Second World War itself.

With the rise of Stalin the bohemianism of the early regime was sloughed off completely; the totalitarianism of the Stalin regime was to survive Stalin's death for decades.

The new Soviet patriotism—quite distinct from Marxist ideology—was reflected in the unprecedented subsidizing of the intelligentsia as a class. Having realized, no doubt, that a disaffected intelligentsia is the most dangerous single social element, the Stalin regime simultaneously straitjacketed and coddled its tame intellectuals. Combining the classic incentives of bribery and fear, it created a general mold for the expression of all artistic and intellectual interests.

The managers of the state economy—*apparatchiki*—increased by leaps and bounds. In 1926 they were numbered at about 2 million, in 1937 9 million, in 1940 11 million and by 1949 between 15 and 16 million. If one recalls that the general tendency of the regime has been to soft-pedal the ramifications of the "apparatus-people," the specific weight of the bureaucracy in Soviet society is obviously substantial.

Concomitantly, the Soviet differentiation in wages became even more acute than in free-enterprise countries, including the United States. Though the apparatus at this time accounted for only 14 percent of the working population, their share of the country's wages was estimated at 35 percent, while the corresponding figures were 33 percent for the workers, who comprise 22 percent of the population, and 29 percent for the peasants, who comprised 53 percent. As for those in the forced labor camps, supposedly about 11 percent of the population, they received only 2 or 3 percent.

In world politics the existence of the Soviet Union was surely a dynamic factor in the preparations for the Second World War, and was, indeed, the vital principle in the organization of

Hitlerism—a reaction both to German distress after the First World War and more specifically to the fears of Bolshevism rampant after the establishment of the neo-Bolshevik state.

But the Soviet Executive itself played an altogether minor role in world affairs before the Second World War. The trickles of refugees that followed the initial repression of non-Bolshevik currents in the early twenties had no effect whatever on politics; nor did the Communist Parties that seceded from the Social-Democratic Parties in Europe in the wake of the Bolshevik putsch and were organized in 1919 under the Third International exert a positive influence of their own. Still less did the various Bolshevik oppositions succeed in influencing their handfuls of followers in the European working-class movement.

Whatever had been the apocalyptic perspective of the early neo-Bolshevik regime, it soon evaporated. The political turmoil in Europe, which after the First World War seemed to favor the emergence of potentially insurrectionary situations—Germany, Hungary, Bulgaria—was altogether beyond the powers of the enfeebled and distracted neo-Bolshevik government to influence. Lenin was obliged to forget his revolutionary euphoria by 1923; the neo-Bolshevik regime accommodated itself to its isolation.

As the imminence of an auxiliary revolution in Europe receded, the various local Communist Parties were automatically transformed into instruments of the neo-Bolshevik state. Hence the tactics of any given national party were no longer seen in the increasingly chimerical perspective of a revolution but through the prism of neo-Bolshevik self-interest.

The most dramatic example of this was the celebrated People's Front before the Second World War and its numerous parallels since.

The neo-Bolshevik regime and the Comintern had clung, if not to their hopes, at least to their intransigent tactics throughout the twenties, but after the disappointment of one revolutionary hope after another in Germany, and with the emergence of the Nazi movement, the regime was confronted by an unmistakable foreshadowing of catastrophe when Hitler came to power in 1933.

The Nazi movement had been successful, after all, for two reasons: Stalin's rejection of any collaboration with the German Social-Democrats in order to forestall Hitler, and Hitler's foreign policy of "eastward expansion"—i.e., the destruction of the Soviet Union—which had secured the tacit, but effective, support of influential circles in Great Britain and France.

Hitler's foreign policy was plainly the gravest danger ever faced by the neo-Bolshevik regime, which now completely reversed its intransigence *vis-à-vis* all capitalist regimes and more particularly its Social-Democratic rivals. The Soviet government launched a largely successful campaign to unite all liberal and socialist elements against the growing threat of the Nazis.

But while the rise of Nazi Germany alarmed Western Europe and even, to some extent, the United States, it did not alarm it seriously enough to give the Stalin regime any assurance against an attack by a rearmed Germany. In August 1939 Stalin abruptly reversed positions and made a pact with Hitler that triggered the Second World War.

What was, perhaps, astonishing in the context of this period was not Stalin's mistrust of the countries that were shortly to become Allies—Great Britain and France—but his serene trust, as it seems, in Hitler's good faith *vis-à-vis* himself. He was, indeed, altogether gullible about Hitler—he greatly admired his brains and dash—and did nothing to alert the Soviet armed forces even when told of an imminent Nazi attack in 1941.

The Hitler-Stalin pact led to the partition of Poland, extinguished as a sovereign state for the fourth time. The Soviet regime adopted a new role as "gatherer of Russian soil" and the executor of ancient Russian claims. The eastern territories of Poland, part of the ancient Kievan realm, had been regained by Catherine the Great by the first Polish partition of 1772; the territories, a bone of contention during the reign of Alexander I, were forcibly detached from the Tsarist Empire by the First World War, and now they were integrated with Soviet Russia, as were the Baltic States and Bessarabia in 1940. The Soviet Union was creeping back to the old borders of Tsarism; the Versailles settlement of 1919 was nullified.

Hitler intended the pact to secure Germany's eastern flank and thus avoid the terrifying prospect of a war on two fronts, the undoing of Hohenzollern Germany twenty-five years before. In the event, however, Hitler was bound to perceive that even a successful assault on Great Britain, even after the occupation of France in 1940, would leave Germany defenseless against the Soviet Union. Thus, in the summer of 1941 the German army flung the bulk of its strength against the Soviet Union.

The Stalin regime was now forced to accept Great Britain as an ally, and for that matter France and a little later the United States as well.

In the beginning the German army did remarkably well; by the end of 1941 it controlled about 40 percent of the total population of the Soviet Union in an area containing 65 percent of its prewar coal production, 68 percent of its pig iron, 58 percent of its steel, 38 percent of its grain, and 84 percent of its sugar, as well as about 40 percent of the railway network. Between June and November, Soviet industrial production had fallen by more than half and steel production by more than two-thirds.

In December 1941, however, there was a setback outside Moscow that proved fateful for the Nazi campaign in Russia. The advance on Moscow had been delayed for a month or two by army difficulties in Yugoslavia. It was finally launched in the coldest winter in memory, with the troops lacking even adequate clothing. The German army was halted.

This was its first serious defeat. Within a few days Hitler made two catastrophic decisions: he declared war on the United States and set in train the "Final Solution" of the "Jewish Question."

Militarily, both decisions were incomprehensible: The German armed forces were incapable of affecting the United States, while the attempt to exterminate the Jews required thousands of SS-men, the equivalent of several divisions, and vast amounts of rolling-stock, vital for the army in Russia, to corral scattered, unarmed Jewish civilians and transport them to death centers in Poland. Thus the attempted extinction of the Jews—between five and six million were killed—served a counter-military purpose.

Moreover, the many sources of Soviet disunity—from religious hostility to the Communist regime to the peasants' hatred of the collective farms—were disregarded by the Nazis in the grip of their obsession about the Slavic "submen." The utter inflexibility of agencies such as the Waffen-SS in their treatment of Russians, Ukrainians, and Poles, made it impossible for the Germans to benefit by any nonmilitary factor. The fabulous mass surrenders of the Russian armies during the first six months of the German onslaught, which should have indicated the internal weaknesses of the Soviet regime, were disregarded.

The disastrous siege of Stalingrad in 1942 undid the German forces completely.

By December 1941 the Japanese attack on Pearl Harbor put the United States directly into the war; as the vast amounts of all kinds of supplies were increased still further, the Russians gradually began moving westward again.

The Nazis had captured Vlasov, a Soviet general sincerely hostile to the Stalin regime. In 1943 the Nazis had almost one million Russians serving in the German army, but they were hesitant about using Vlasov, no doubt because he was a Russian patriot and opposed to the atomization of Russia planned by the Nazi geopoliticians even as their own realm was melting away. Halfheartedly accepted in November 1944, Vlasov was allowed to proclaim a "manifesto," highlighted by a demand to overthrow Stalinist tyranny and "to liberate the people of our homeland from the Bolshevik system."

The Vlasov army was not allowed more than a few divisions, an indication of persistent German mistrust. Vlasov was smothered in the converging Soviet and American advances. Interned by the Americans in Prague, he was handed over to the Russians and executed in 1946.

The Soviet Union emerged from the ruins of the war in a commanding international position. Its ability to withstand the German onslaught, even though with the massive aid of the United States and Great Britain, and to make a westward advance with its own armies enhanced its prestige, which was bolstered by the political incapacity of the United States administration and its insistence on fighting the war from a purely military point of view. This astigmatism not only made the American leaders go out of their way to allow the Soviet armies to take Berlin, Prague, and Vienna, but enshrined these artificial military positions in a series of diplomatic accords.

The Yalta Conference in February 1945 granted the Soviet Union a dominant position in the Far East, which an American occupation of Japan could balance only partly, and in the whole of Eastern Europe except Greece. Although some compromises were effected at Potsdam in the summer of 1945, the net result was favorable to the Soviet Union's interpretation of the accords reached in Yalta and in Teheran in the winter of 1943. Soviet territory was extended by about 193,000 square miles; not only were the Baltic countries altogether absorbed, but the Soviet Union also engulfed eastern Poland and Bessarabia, north Bukovina, the northern part of eastern Prussia, and parts of Finland. Moreover, an impressive array of buffer states was established on Soviet initiative. Poland, East Germany, Czechoslovakia, Hungary, Bulgaria, Rumania, and for a time Yugoslavia and Albania immediately became satellites. Soviet gains came to a total of roughly 110 million people.

By 1945 the Soviet regime, propped up by the "bastion of world capitalism," the United States, whose administration had been intensively penetrated by Soviet intelligence, was at the zenith of its authority—far above its nadir in 1938. Its troops were in Berlin and Vienna, had come as far as the Elbe, controlled a third of Germany, the Danube area and the Balkans as a whole, and had occupied Manchuria.

These spectacular political successes were a dramatic counterpoint to the material devastation of the war, which was on a scale comparable with the havoc of the First World War and the subsequent civil war. The total loss of life in the Soviet Union was estimated at about 20 million, the homeless numbered some 25 million. Countless towns had been levelled; the housing shortage was catastrophic.

The material losses were made up for by the harnessing of the industrial power of the satellites. Soviet control of East Germany secured 36 percent of Germany's 1936 industrial capacity, for instance; the system of reparations between the Soviet Union and the satellites was heavily weighted in favor of the former. Incalculable assets streamed into the Soviet Union; German talents of all kinds, including nuclear physicists, were imported wholesale.

The Second World War—known in the Soviet Union as the Fatherland War—greatly intensified Stalin's prewar tendency to amplify Soviet patriotism through the incorporation of traditional Russian motifs. In November 1941, in a speech Stalin made to the troops in Moscow under the threat of the German guns, he had struck a note characteristic of the whole Soviet war. Disregarding the Communist pantheon altogether, he had held aloft the "virile images of our great ancestors—Nevsky, Donskoy, Minin, Pozharsky, Suvorov, and Kutuzov."

Brandishing before his listeners' eyes the ikons of Imperial Russia, Stalin brought Soviet patriotism, kindled during the thirties, to its logical conclusion. He drove the point home at a reception for the Red Army commanders in the Kremlin in 1945; with Germany shattered, he gave a toast, not to the multi-ethnic citizens of the Soviet Union, but to the health of the Russian people—"the outstanding nation among the peoples of the Soviet Union."

The Jewish "problem," which Marxists had claimed would vanish along with traditional society, not only failed to vanish, but even after the conquest of Hitler's Germany was exacerbated and given a specifically "Marxist-Leninist" tincture.

At the end of the forties a campaign was launched by the neo-Bolshevik Executive specifically aimed at the Jews ("passportless wanderers" and "rootless cosmopolitans"). This embedded deep in Soviet life the classical theme of formal, medieval anti-Semitism, a theme that was articulated, amplified and institutionalized in a series of satellite "Show Trials" (in Hungary, Bulgaria, and Czechoslovakia) in the late forties and fifties, where lifelong Bolsheviks, expressly denounced as Jews, and for that matter as Zionists, were stigmatized on the model of the Moscow Show Trials, as agents of a "capitalist" restoration and servants of the principal enemies of the Soviet regime.

In 1953 Stalin was on the verge, as was to come out, of preparing a new Show Trial, heralded by the intensively publicized charges that some well-known Soviet physicians—nearly all Jews, as was equally publicized—were engaged in a plot against him and the Politburo. Then he died in circumstances regarded by many as suspicious.

The death of Stalin, without question the most powerful individual in history, not only marked the end of the era associated with his name—though interpretations of this have been very various—but the end of the Stalin cult as such.

His death naturally led to some backstage maneuvering at the summits of the all-powerful Party. Since there was no legal,

Stalin died on March 5, 1953. Here he lies in state, surrounded by leading party mourners. Group on the left, l. to r.: Molotov, his ardent supporter, now exiled as ambassador to Outer Mongolia; Voroshilov, a mere figurehead for many years, now retired; Beria, dreaded head of Stalin's police, hastily executed after his master's death; Malenkov, demoted to an obscure technical position after a brief period heading the Soviet hierarchy. Group on the right, l. to r.: Bulganin, eclipsed after a stretch of public celebrity; Khrushchov, now the master; Kaganovitch, pensioned off and retired; Mikoyan, wizard of Soviet commerce, still important today.

still less doctrinal, justification for making the office of General Secretary supreme, there was no institutional framework for the contest between the top luminaries of the Party: this created a vacuum filled by primitive power politics.

Nikita Khrushchev, made First Secretary (not General Secretary, still too close to Stalin) of the Central Committee in September 1953, was to oust his rivals and become Party leader a few years later. He attempted some major organizational reforms, with the usual failure inherent in the problem. One of his macrocosmic successes, however, was brought about in May 1955, when he made a trip to Belgrade for discussions with Tito. Whether or not the breakaway of Yugoslavia from the Soviet camp in 1948 had been genuine, after these discussions it rejoined, semi-clandestinely, the Soviet bloc. This may have been linked to a policy initiated by

232

Khrushchev, the formation of an overall disinformation project taking in all intelligence services of the Soviet bloc, for the purpose of allowing some latitude to individual regimes while misleading Western allies by simulations of conflicts.

Khrushchev, at a secret session of the 20th Party Congress (February 1956), officially exploded the Stalin myth once and for all. In copious detail Khrushchev, overcome by emotion, bitterly attacked Stalin's megalomania, sadism, cowardice, and incompetence. For seven hours he aired in public charges that among opponents of the regime had been commonplace for decades. Lay opinion was startled; for a time faithful Communists everywhere were paralyzed by doubt. The pious, who had actually believed the illusions manufactured by neo-Bolshevik propaganda, were naturally upset by the abrupt annihilation of the orderly mythical world a whole generation had grown up in.

But even the shattering revelations of Khrushchev in February 1956 dealt only with the Party victims: the vast slaughters of the population (in which Khrushchev himself had played a stellar role) were untouched. Khrushchev made much of the systematic falsification of history, which had been written by Stalin personally or on his orders (Stalin had once said "paper will stand for anything"). In short, Khrushchev denounced the whole "cult of personality" but succeeded, characteristically, in slanting his denunciations away from the Party that had brought Stalin into being. (The very phrase "cult of personality"—picked up from one of Marx's letters—is a typical neo-Bolshevik euphemism.)

The 20th Party Congress of 1956, perhaps as part of the new overall disinformation policy, modified a celebrated formula made much of by both Lenin and Stalin: that war between the

Soviet Union and the West was inevitable. It was laid down at the Congress that while war was, to be sure, inevitable, it was not "fatalistically" so.

The effects of Khrushchev's "secret speech" and the attendant initiation of a de-Stalinization campaign had intensified general discontent and considerable erosion of the central authority. In the Soviet Union itself many intellectuals and young people channeled their indignation into active agitation that went beyond mere grumbling. The denunciation of Stalin inevitably led beyond Stalin.

Abroad, the Soviet stranglehold on Eastern Europe was shaken: In October 1956 heavy detachments of Soviet troops were hastily sent into Hungary to put down an uprising that was in fact led by Communists acting as workers' leaders. In Poland, too, military intervention, which had been looming, was averted by an accord with Wladyslaw Gomulka, who had become leader once again over Soviet objections.

The crushing of the Hungarian rebellion by Soviet troops in October and November of 1956 coincided with an acceleration of the Soviet penetration of the Middle East.

Initially a sponsor of the newly established State of Israel in 1948, the Soviet regime almost immediately changed its tactic and switched over to overt and increasingly dynamic support of the various claims made by Israel's uniformly hostile neighbors.

It was perhaps inevitable for the Soviet Union to take advantage of the internal ferment within the various Arabic-speaking countries bordering the State of Israel. Without doing much more than responding to invitations, the Soviet Executive could intervene massively in the 1956 Sinai War conducted by Great Britain, France, and Israel against Egypt and in consequence secure a foothold in Egypt, Syria, and Iraq that it could exploit for its own purposes.

Though it acted in concert with the United States in obliging Israel to give up its territorial gains in the 1956 Sinai War, the Soviet Executive soon resumed an independent strategy. In 1967 it backed very heavily a coalition of Egypt, Syria, and Jordan against the State of Israel. When the Israelis managed to withstand and in fact crush the Egyptian and Syrian armies, the very discomfiture of the Arab forces interacted with Soviet discomfiture itself in anchoring the Soviet Executive even more firmly in the Middle East.

This procedure was repeated in the autumn of 1973, when Egypt and Syria were even more powerfully armed by the Soviet Union, which moreover compensated for the astonishingly swift attrition of armaments by fabulously expensive sophisticated armaments of its own. In the Yom Kippur War the difference was that the Egyptian and Syrian forces acquitted themselves far better than in 1967. Moreover, the oil embargo, proclaimed at the same time by the oil-rich Arab states in the Persian Gulf, quickly outweighed the territorial aspects of the war itself.

Under Khrushchev a rupture seemed to take place between the Soviet Union and Red China: the two major components of the vast Marxist-Leninist bloc seemed to be diverging. It is true that relations between the Kremlin and the movement led by Mao Zedong had been ambiguous from the outset. Immediately after the 1917 putsch the prospects of a Chinese revolution seemed very bright to the euphoric Bolsheviks: they were sympathetic to the Chinese nationalist movement, with which a working alliance was achieved after the civil war in Russia. During the twenties, on Stalin's initiative, the Chinese nationalist organization, the Kuomintang, was fully supported, perhaps in an effort to compensate for the disastrous setbacks of the communist movement in Europe. The Soviet Executive agreed not to build up the Chinese Communist Party, founded in 1921, independently of the Kuomintang but to support the Kuomintang directly.

However, after the death of Sun Yat-sen in 1925 and the rise of Chiang Kai-shek, the situation changed abruptly. Chiang Kai-shek, now head of the Kuomintang, broke the pact Stalin had been nurturing against the attacks of various opposition elements in the Party, and by a ruthless massacre of Communists and industrial workers in April 1927 brought the collaboration between the two movements to an end.

When the Chinese Communists, headed by Mao Zedong and Chou En-lai, succeeded, after overcoming the Japanese army and expelling Chiang Kai-shek's forces, in establishing themselves in 1948 as the sole power in mainland China, both Mao Zedong and Stalin disregarded in public their differences of the past and proclaimed their solidarity as Marxists.

In January 1968 the emergence in Czechoslovakia of a new leader, Alexander Dubcek, led the "Prague Spring," an optimistic attempt to give communism a human face. By the summer this was cut short: Soviet forces, including East German, Polish, Hungarian and Bulgarian detachments occupied Czechoslovakia, reimposing the iron discipline from the center.

The Czech invasion had two fairly long-range effects—the Brezhnev Doctrine, which meant that the Soviet Union would, if necessary, intervene militarily in the affairs of its satellites, a fact obvious from the very beginning, and it also put a stop to the hopes of détente, the Soviet goal, as it would have seemed, since the mid-1960s. It was to be another decade or two before détente became a serious perspective in relations between the Soviet Union and the West.

The suppression of the Prague Spring intensified repression everywhere; it also took in cultural life. Solzhenitsyn, who had been seriously constricted even before the invasion of Czechoslovakia (his manuscripts had been confiscated and some of his published works withdrawn), was expelled from the Writers' Union in November 1969.

The Helsinki Conference of the summer of 1975 sealed the territorial settlement concluding the Second World War, at least *vis-à-vis* the Soviet Union. It was a clear-cut victory for the Soviet Executive, which got the approval of all powers for its own borders in Europe and Asia in return for its lavishly distributed promises of high regard for human rights and freedom.

In that same summer the Soviet Executive embarked on an extensive military/political program in Africa, beginning in Angola and coinciding with the cooling of interest in the U. S. government, after the disappointing outcome of the Vietnam War, in further involvements abroad.

Making use of the manpower of its wholly-subsidized Cuban satellite, as well as some personnel from East Germany, the Soviet Executive airlifted heavy weapons to Angola, six thousand miles away from its borders, then proceeded to the establishment of strongpoints throughout Africa (Ethiopia, Namibia, Somaliland) and in the Arabian Peninsula (Aden).

In 1973, at a secret conference of Party heads in Eastern Europe, Brezhnev predicted that by the mid-eighties the "will of the Kremlin would prevail throughout the world." On the eve of the massive strategic undertaking, camouflaged for the purposes of the world media by the use of non-Soviet troops and technical personnel, this prediction might well have seemed plausible.

Leonid Brezhnev, after eighteen years of peace, died in November 1982. He was succeeded by a former head of the KGB, Yuri Andropov, who at the age of 72 set about coping with the red tape, corruption and pervasive inefficiency of the vast Soviet bureaucracy. Andropov died the following year; he was succeeded by Konstantin Chernenko, 76, a bureaucratic routineer.

The second Soviet generation—men in their seventies—had come to an end.

CHAPTER XI

THE NEW COURSE

During the euphoria that attended the victory of the neo-Bolshevik dictatorship over the Nazi regime in the Second World War, the prospect of at last realizing the optimistic slogan of the regime, "to overtake and pass America," might have seemed realistic. Stalin's stubborn rejection of economic aid from the United States, due no doubt to fear of American power, might well have seemed mere prudence.

The Soviet Union, unique in history as claiming the support of an ideal theory for its conduct as a real political entity, derived remarkable benefits from that fact alone. The socialism flaunted by the regime was effective, at least for purposes of propaganda. Socialism in an ideal form had a potent appeal to embryo dictatorships and to elite conspiracies throughout the former colonial areas of the world—what became known, in the wake of the Second World War, as the Third World.

The Soviet regime became a model for elite strivers in backward areas. In Latin America and Africa, especially, Marxist-Leninist, i.e., pro-Soviet recruits drawn from the middle and upper classes proliferated. In these areas, where free-enterprise was under the constriction of particularly retrograde parochial leaders, it was natural for eager young men to be seduced by the prospect of seizing power under the banner of revolution. All this, following the model of Soviet totalitarianism itself, was expressed in one form or another of Marxist ideology.

Daily life in Moscow: the personality cult no longer applies to Stalin, but every day delegations and tourists from all over the USSR queue patiently through Red Square to visit Lenin's mausoleum.

An influential factor in shaping public opinion outside the Soviet bloc was the remarkable phenomenon of a pro-Soviet shift among important elements of the great Christian Churches. The Bolshevik *putsch* in 1917, which had the appearance of a peaceful victory won by a Marxist socialist party, naturally inflamed opponents, but at the same time the grandiose aim of the Bolsheviks—reform of the world—had an immediate effect on many Protestants and Catholics in the West, despite the notorious atheism of Marx and his followers. After the Second World War, Marxism as such exercised a magnetic attraction for important branches not only of the great Protestant confederations but also of the Roman Catholic Church. Colloquies between Marxists and Dominicans, Franciscans and Jesuits became common; in the sixties "Liberation Theology," a powerful synthesis between primitive Christianity and primitive Marxism, became an international force of some utility to the geopolitical plans of the neo-Bolshevik Executive.

The political defeat suffered by the United States after its military success in Vietnam had no doubt created a favorable climate of opinion, especially in the American media. An intensification of conspiratorial techniques was the only way out: a vast program of subversion and penetration in Latin America, Africa, and Asia, especially in the Middle East, was implemented with remarkable success.

The absorption of Cuba into the Soviet network created a prop for numerous adventures in Africa, where 50,000 soldiers armed with machine-guns could be a decisive force. The heavy subsidization of the African National Congress, and its presentation as an inevitable alternative to the white South African government, the establishment of actual Marxist-Leninist regimes in countries as far apart from each other as

Angola and Ethiopia, the creation of a whole network of puppets indicated the flexibility and thrust of these Soviet initiatives. In the Middle East, too, the Soviet Executive solved the problem of Muslim fronts as easily as it had found Christian fronts in the West.

These Muslim fronts were the principal channel of such machinations in the Middle East. They were all very naturally allied against both the State of Israel and to a large extent against the United States. In this strategy the Soviet Executive enjoys, of course, the support of the many universalist Jews who themselves are willing tools, agents or allies of the neo-Bolshevik Executive against both Israel and the United States.

On the higher levels of psychological warfare the framework of the contest between Russia and the United States— the Cold War—was grounded in the simple device of nuclear blackmail deployed with such effectiveness during the 1962 Cuban missile crisis. The Soviet Executive found it child's play to exploit the sensibilities of ordinary people by holding aloft these two alternatives: all Soviet geopolitical advances— the puppetization of Cuba, Nicaragua, Ethiopia, Angola, and ultimately South Africa—were submerged in a cloud of misapplied apprehension.

Other campaigns were going equally well: The South African government was besieged as no government had been before. The well-nigh universal disapproval of apartheid— racial segregation in national elections, housing areas, etc.— was used by the neo-Bolshevik Executive as the basis of a broad campaign to undermine, in its own interests, the South African government. The oddity of this preoccupation with the vote, which Soviet citizens had not had since 1917, was

242

noticed by few, just as the actual massacres in other African countries—notably Ethiopia—were paid scarcely any attention at all.

Russian policy in the Middle East was highlighted from the sixties on by a simple objective—to get the United States out of the Persian Gulf. For this the Muslim fronts were indispensable. All the Muslim fronts, by taking hostages well-nigh at random, by inciting genuine massacres that made the whole area comprising Syria and Lebanon an impenetrable jungle of murderous intrigues and butcheries, had this objective—to convince America that the Middle East was utterly unmanageable, and that the only practical thing to do was to get out.

By the end of the eighties, in short, it might well have seemed that the neo-Bolshevik Executive, relentlessly squeezing its people, had established itself as a superpower by creating an impressive nuclear arsenal on the one hand, and on the other an equally impressive network of Marxist-Leninist allies and agents.

Under the neo-Bolsheviks, the peasantry had been for all practical purposes wiped out; the forced collectivization at the beginning of the thirties, after killing off millions of peasants, had been followed gradually and then after the Second World War torrentially by a mass exodus to the towns and cities.

The older generation could no longer do the hard work of farming, the middle-aged and younger people had largely left. The greatest granary in the world, up to the Bolshevik *putsch*, could no longer feed itself.

In sum, a total of tens of millions of people had been killed for political reasons during the decade 1929–39. These losses, plus the absence of what would have been their progeny, had brought about a shortage in the Soviet population, since the last published census at the time of the First World War, of about 100 million.

From the Second World War on the economy was merely tinkered with; minor concessions were made, withdrawn, made again, etc. The problems of the economy seemed to be linked to the very fact of state management in economies that by and large remained stubbornly backward. The quarter-billion people under the neo-Bolshevik Executive—together with the billion-plus under the Chinese Communist Party—could no longer, it seemed, be held down by the bureaucracy: three-quarters of a century of regimentation in the Soviet Union, half a century of the same in China, had proved incapable of suppressing discontent. The fundamental inability of these state-run economies to provide anything in the way of consumer goods had finally, in a seismic surge, forced its way into the awareness of the self-appointed leaders.

Hope for a real change sprang up once again. Since Stalin's death in 1953, to be sure, this hope had been springing up regularly; each and every successor of his gave rise to a state of euphoria in the throngs of the hopeful and in the great media of the West. The disappointment would be followed, again and again, by a reformulation of projected mini-reforms.

By the eighties, with the intensification of technological advances in the wake of the Second World War, the neo-Bolshevik regime was entirely eliminated as a contender in the competition of the great centers of the world—the United States, the looming European Common Market and Japan, and even the smaller free-enterprise states of Eastern Asia—Taiwan, South Korea, Singapore.

Two aspects of the health and physical strength cult as expressed today in the Soviet Union. Above, in the Moscow central telegraph office, operators go through physical culture movements.

Nor could its outdistancing be concealed from its subjects: the unavoidable necessity of educating its population made it impossible to make the Marxist-Leninist cocoon of ideas watertight: intelligent people at universities could not be immunized against the flood of diversified information permeating all the technical fields of the modern world—electronics, computerology, sophisticated engineering of all kinds.

By the end of the eighties, in fact, it had become clear that the Marxist-Leninist regimes could not maintain their congealed bureaucracies. The dissatisfaction was so pervasive that it was no longer possible to govern even by means of the bloodshed the population had gotten used to in Russia in the twenties and thirties. The military cadres could not be counted on for any large-scale repressions; the ardor of the nucleus itself was contaminated, perhaps, by deep doubts as to the point of it all. The simple-minded fanaticism, plus desperation of the early neo-Bolsheviks had been corroded beyond recall.

At the same time it was obvious that the success of the Soviet policy of worldwide subversion and infiltration could not serve to eliminate the United States as an obstacle to neo-Bolshevik world hegemony. The achievements in Latin America—Cuba, Nicaragua—and the strong-points established in Africa and Asia were peripheral, after all.

In the middle of the eighties, accordingly, a new course for the neo-Bolshevik bloc electrified world politics.

The new course was spear-headed by a rising star, Mikhail Gorbachov, who in March 1985 became head of the Soviet government. The fanfare in the media focused on the reforms implied by his key concepts—"perestroika" and "glasnost" (roughly "restructuring" and "openness").

Gorbachov's dramatic appearance seemed to be a response to a period of disturbance through Soviet-occupied Europe, beginning with Poland, from 1981 on, and echoing throughout the satellites. In 1989 Poland, the Baltic States, Czechoslovakia, East Germany, Hungary, Bulgaria and Rumania were to begin agitation for independence of the Soviet Union in some degree.

Borders were opened between East and West Germany, as well as between Austria, Hungary and Czechoslovakia; the Berlin Wall was opened up and torn down; people began moving about more or less freely. All the satellite governments began appointing non-Communist members; free elections were held out for the fairly near future.

The media hailed these events with joy; still, the process was not so straightforward as it appeared.

If the free elections were not yet held, while non-Communists were already being "appointed," it was blatantly obvious that those doing the appointing were the Communists themselves.

It is obvious, in fact, that the Soviet Executive had instructed the various satellite Communist Parties running the governments to slacken restraints. The tumultuous elation that ensued was entirely foreseeable.

Yet Gorbachov's first major speech in Moscow (3 November 1987) was entirely disconcerting: at the very moment of sounding what was evidently meant to be a clarion call for reform, he embarked on a lengthy excursion into the dinosaur past of the neo-Bolshevik Party—a denunciation of "Trotskyism." Thus the great achievement of Stalin's statecraft—a powerful formula for satanizing all forms of dissent—was resurrected a half-century after its purpose had been achieved.

Gorbachov's statements rotated around a fundamental contradiction, soared over by the media and most commentators. While agreeing that Soviet society could realize its potential only by opening itself up to "freedom" and "democracy," he also kept saying flatly, at various times, that while freedom and democracy would be striven for there would be no return to large-scale private property, that the Party monopoly would not vanish in the play of pluralistic politics, nor would "communist principles" be abandoned.

Through the turmoil in the satellites and in the Soviet Union it was evident that the long-range goals of the Soviet

Executive remained untouched. The lavish subsidies propping up Cuba were dropped, though the subsidy to the African National Congress went on. Dropping, or suspending the use of the Sandinistas in Nicaragua may be considered the sacrifice of a pawn to sustain the desired impression.

It was evident, indeed, that the neo-Bolshevik Executive's original objective, epitomized by the abandonment in the sixties of the slogan "to overtake and pass America" and its replacement by planetary subversion through penetration and proxies, had survived the uncontrollable collapse of the economy. The very fact of conspicuous economic incapacity was turned into a strategic-diplomatic instrument for the ultimate circumventing of America. The public-relations campaign carried on by Gorbachov and his colleagues, if successful, would persuade the West that the elimination of any danger of war, long since superseded, entailed a natural prospect for peaceful reconstruction on all levels.

The aim of the Gorbachov reform movement, in short, was to present a plausible picture of its economic problems and secure a political benefit from them by persuading the United States government that even though Soviet armaments, throughout all negotiations about "arms control," had grown more formidable than ever, the *intentions* of the neo-Bolshevik Executive were now transformed.

By the beginning of the nineties this became the leitmotif of world affairs. It was buttressed by the media, particularly in the United States, which from the very outset molded public reception of the theme by constant repetition of a few basic concepts, absorbed by the government as well as by the public.

The pre-war drive towards the mechanization of industry, already intensive, has been resumed at an accelerated pace.

The demonstration of this change of heart in the neo-Bolshevik Executive revolved around the claim that the agitation against the Communist government of the Soviet satellites was a spontaneous upheaval of the masses, provoked by the universal yearning for the creature comforts denied them so long by shortcomings of the planned economy. The corollary of this was the thirst for democracy.

And the crowning proof to this change of heart was the good grace with which the Soviet Executive had accepted the spontaneous upheaval, and even endorsed the same goals.

The transformation of intentions in the neo-Bolshevik Executive was illustrated by countless reports that the Russian economy was on its last legs: reports of commodity shortages, notorious since the Bolshevik putsch in 1917, surfaced again in force. The impression was given that the authorities, yielding to the craving for consumer goods, were now obliged to rectify the economy.

Yet to make this view plausible a very obvious fact had to be bypassed—that the agitation for goods, for democracy, for freedom of movement, had in fact been instigated by the neo-Bolshevik Executive itself, and would, indeed, have been inconceivable otherwise.

Countless clichés ran riot in the wake of the Gorbachov talk about reforms: "Communism is crumbling . . . Marxism is dead . . . the Soviet Union is feeble . . . the planned economy is a shambles . . . the Soviet Union needs help . . . armaments can now be cut back . . . peace will bring its dividend. . . ."

Yet the plausibility of these clichés was undermined by two confusions: one was that the neo-Bolshevik authorities were preoccupied by consumer deprivation, the second was that Marxism was still an integral element of the neo-Bolshevik state.

These men marching with rifles are trained to use devastating atomic weapons.

It is true, of course, that the ideological underpinnings of the neo-Bolshevik dictatorship had always been rooted, officially, in Marxism. Hundreds of millions of school-children were subjected after the 1917 putsch to the complex of Marxist themes ("dialectical materialism" etc.), but by the time of Khrushchov the leaders were too sophisticated for their traditional Marxism.

The purpose of the huge charade set in motion by the Gorbachov coterie can be grasped merely by discerning its penultimate goal—to demonstrate that the formidable dimensions of its armaments were irrelevant because of the change of heart of the regime, now converted to capitalism.

The end of the century is beginning to be celebrated with growing intensity as the beginning of the new millenium; the Russian leaders have begun enlightening the world with their conception of the true point of the European Union, i.e., its role in their campaign against the nation-state, along with their general plan to eject the United States from both the Middle East and from Europe.

Their essential understanding of "capitalism," as well as what the word means to those powerful individuals for whom the word means no more than a synonym for a traditional form of economic piracy, has begun to be clarified in practice.

In what may be the final or semi-final shape of the Russian government—i.e., the form in which the power of the top cliques is expressed—it seems safe to say that any form of Russian "capitalism" will be handled "bureaucratically," that is, politically, as before by those in the inner core via the manipulation of whatever symbolic devices become effective in the evolution of the tight dictatorship in its super-modern shape.

BIBLIOGRAPHY

Baykov, Alexander. *The Development of the Soviet Economic System,* Cambridge: 1946.

Buchanan, G. *My Mission to Russia,* 2 vols., London: 1923.

Bunyan, J., and Fisher, H. H. *The Bolshevik Revolution 1917–18,* Stanford: 1934.

Carmichael, Joel. *Stalin's Masterpiece,* New York and London: 1974.

———*Trotsky,* New York and London: 1974.

Chamberlin, W. H. *The Russian Revolution,* 2 vols., New York: 1960.

Conquest, Robert. *The Great Terror,* London and New York: 1968.

Dan, Theodor. *The Origins of Bolshevism,* translated by J. Carmichael, New York and London: 1965.

Dubnov, S. M. *History of the Jews in Russia and Poland,* 3 vols., Philadelphia: 1916–1920.

Florinsky, Michael T. *Russia: A History and an Interpretation,* 2 vols., New York: 1947, 1953.

Gankin, O. H., and Fischer, H. H. *The Bolsheviks and the World War,* Stanford: 1940.

Golitsyn, Anatoliy. *New Lies for Old,* New York: 1984.

Grebing, H. *Politische Studien,* Munich: 1957.

Haffner, Sebastian. *Anmerkungen zu Hitler,* Munich: 1978.

Heller, Mikhail, and Nekrich, Aleksandr M. *Utopia in Powe: The History of the Soviet Union from 1917 to the Present,* New York: 1986.

Katkov, George. *Russia 1917: The February Revolution,* New York: 1967.

Kerensky, Alexander. *The Catastrophe,* London: 1927.

Kliuchevsky, V. O. *Kurs russkoi istorii (Lectures in Russian History),* 5 vols., Petrograd: 1904–21. Republished Moscow: 1936.

Knox, A. *With the Russian Army, 1914–1917,* 2 vols., New York: 1921.

Kovalevsky, Pierre. *Manuel d'histoire russe,* Paris: 1948.

Lenin, V. I. *Sochineniya,* Vols. I–XXXV, 4th ed., Moscow: 1941–50.

Lockhart, Bruce. *Memoirs of a British Agent,* New York and London: 1932.

Ludendorff, Erich. *Meine Kriegserinnerungen, 1914–18,* Berlin: 1919.

Martin, Malachi. *The Jesuits,* New York: 1987.

Masaryk, T. G. *The Spirit of Russia,* London: 1918.

Maynard, J. *The Russian Peasant,* London: 1942.

Milyukov, P. N., Seignobos, C., and Eisenmann, L. *Histoire de Russie,* 3 vols., Paris: 1933.

Milyukov, P. N. *Ocherki po istorii russkoi kul'tury (Essays in the History of Russian Culture),* Rev. ed., 3 vols. in 4, Paris: 1930–37.

——*Istoriya Vtoroy Russkoi revolyutsii,* Sofia: 1921.

Mirsky, Prince S. D. *Russia: A Social History,* London: 1931.

——*Contemporary Russian Literature, 1881–1925,* New York: 1927.

Nicolaevsky, B. I. *Power and the Soviet Elite,* New York: 1965.

Orlov, Alexander. *The Secret History of Stalin's Crimes,* London: 1953.

Rauch, Georg von. *A History of Soviet Russia,* New York: 1957.

Sadoul, Jacques. *Notes sur la révolution bolchévique,* Paris: 1919.

Schapiro, Leonard. *The History of the Communist Party of the Soviet Union,* 2nd ed., New York and London: 1970.

Seton-Watson, Hugh. *The Decline of Imperial Russia,* London: 1952.

Shub, David. *Lenin,* Pelican Edition: 1966.

Stählin, K. *Geschichte Russlands,* 4 vols., Berlin: 1939 (completed).

Sukhanov, N. N. *Zapiski o Revolyutsii,* 7 vols., Berlin: 1922–23. Translated, abridged, and edited as *The Russian Revolution 1917,* by J. Carmichael, London and New York: 1955. New ed. 1975.

Sumner, B. H. *A Short History of Russia,* New York: 1943.

Trotsky, Leon. *History of the Russian Revolution,* 3 vols., London: 1932–33.

Tsereteli, I. G. *Vospominaniya o fevral'skoy revolyutsii,* 2 vols., Paris and The Hague: 1963.

Vernadsky, G. and Karpovich, M. *A History of Russia,* 2 vols., New Haven: 1943–48.

Welter, G. *Histoire de Russie,* Paris: 1949.

Wolfe, Bertram. *Three Who Made a Revolution,* New York: 1948.

Zamoyski, Adam. *The Polish Way,* New York and Toronto: 1988.

Zeman, Z. A. B. (ed.) *Germany and the Revolution in Russia, 1915–18,* London: 1958.

Zeman, Z. A. B., and Scharlau, W. B. *The Merchant of Revolution: The Life of Alexander Israel Helphand* (Parvus), London and New York: 1965.

Other Illustrated History titles from Hippocrene...

IRELAND: AN ILLUSTRATED HISTORY

Henry Weisser

Erin go bragh! While it is easy to appreciate the natural beauty of Ireland, the Emerald Isle's history is also a rich and complex subject of study. Spanning prehistoric and Celtic Ireland to modern times, this concise, illustrated volume examines the people, religion, social changes, and politics that have evolved into the tradition of modern Ireland. Henry Weisser takes the reader on a journey through Ireland's past—to show how historic events have left an indelible mark on everything from architecture and economy, to the spirit and lifestyles of the Irish people.

Henry Weisser received his Ph.D. from Columbia University and is a Professor of History at Colorado State University. He has taught Irish history for many years, and has led groups of students and teachers on trips to Ireland. He is the author of seven books, including *Hippocrene Companion Guide to Ireland, Companion Guide to Britain,* and *U.S.A. Guide to the Rocky Mountain States.*

166 pages—50 illustrations—5 x 7—0-7818-0693-3—W—$11.95hc—(782)

THE CELTIC WORLD:
AN ILLUSTRATED HISTORY
700 B.C. TO THE PRESENT

Patrick Lavin

From the valleys of Bronze Age Urnfielders to the works of 20th century Irish-American literary greats Mary Higgins Clark and Seamus Heaney, Patrick Lavin leads the reader on an entertaining and informative journey through 150 captivating pages of Celtic history, culture, and tradition, including 50 illustrations.

This is a book to be enjoyed by the curious non-specialist; from young scholars to those simply interested in Celtic history, here is the perfect gift idea, a reference guide for travelers, and a wonderfully concise yet extensive and insightful survey of Celtic history.

Patrick Lavin was born in County Roscommon, Ireland. He is a graduate of California State University, Northridge and is retired from service with the United States Government. An avid history enthusiast, he spends his retirement years researching Celtic and Irish history and writing non-fiction books and articles. His works include *Thank You Ireland* (co-author) and *Celtic Ireland: Roots and Routes*. He currently resides in Tucson, Arizona.

150 pages—50 illustrations—5 x 7—0-7818-0731-X—W—$11.95hc—(582)

MEXICO: AN ILLUSTRATED HISTORY

Michael E. Burke

This handy historical guide traces Mexico from the peasant days of the Olmecs to the late 20th century. With over 150 pages and 50 illustrations, the reader discovers how events of Mexico's past have left an indelible mark on the politics, economy, culture, spirit, and growth of this country and its people. Tragedies and triumphs, dependency and conquest, social class and power—all are explored in depth, and are the result of the author's own extensive experience and research in Mexico. Here is an ideal gift volume—perfect for students, travelers, or anyone interested in the customs, heritage and history of Mexico.

Michael Burke is a Professor of History at Villanova University. He is author of *Hippocrene Companion Guide to Mexico.*

150 pages—50 illustrations—5 x 7—0-7818-0690-9—W—$11.95hc—(585)